Introduction to International Studies

Introduction to International Studies

Maurits Berger

LEIDEN UNIVERSITY PRESS

The publication of this volume was made possible by the Faculty of Humanities, Leiden University, the Netherlands, based on a teaching innovation grant.

Cover design: Andre Klijsen
Cover illustration: boti1985
Lay-out: Coco Bookmedia, Amersfoort
Printer: Printforce Nederland B.V.; Culemborg

Every effort has been made to obtain permission to use all copyrighted illustrations reproduced in this book. Nonetheless, whosoever believes to have rights to this material is advised to contact the publisher.

ISBN 9789087284725
e-ISBN 9789400605091 (e-PDF)
e-ISBN 9789400605336 (e-PUB)
https://doi.org/10.24415/9789087284725
NUR 697

Contact EU General Product Safety Regulation (GPSR): productsafety@lup.nl

Contents

PART IV: Global Challenges

Acknowledgements

This textbook is the second in a Leiden University Press series of textbooks on themes and topics in International Studies as taught and studied at Leiden University. This project was initiated by Prof. Isabelle Duyvesteyn when she was chair of the International Studies program, and the project generously provided me with the funds to appoint a student assistant and to pay for the costs of the included graphs and images.

My thanks go out to my colleagues Prof. Isabelle Duyvesteyn, Dr. Jaap Kamphuis and Dr. Jochem van den Boogert, who served as the reading committee for this textbook. They were willing and able to make time in their busy schedules of teaching and managing the Leiden International Studies program and to meticulously read my drafts and provide them with valuable comments. I would also like to extent a warm thank you and eternal gratitude to the anonymous peer reader who reviewed the final manuscript.

The bulk of the work could not have been done without the help of Sara Amraoui, my student-assistant who was always at the ready whenever I needed it. My conversations with her provided me with key insights into the needs and expectations of the future student users of this textbook.

A final word of thanks is for the publisher Saskia Gieling and the editorial coordinator Lisa van Vliet, who gave me the support and assistance to get the job done.

Introduction

International Studies, as defined in this textbook, focus on the issues of today. In my time teaching International Studies, I've had new topical issues to discuss every year: the first year of Donald Trump's presidency in 2017, #MeToo in 2018, worldwide mass protests (in Hong Kong, Iran, Iraq, Lebanon, Sudan, Algeria, Catalonia, Bolivia and Chile) in 2019, Black Lives Matter in 2020, the Covid-19 pandemic in 2021, the invasion of Ukraine by Russia in 2022, the Gaza war in 2023, issues of international law (genocide, occupation and apartheid) in 2024, the American reconfiguration of global relations in 2025. Discussing these issues in a textbook means it is continuously out of date. What this textbook will do, therefore, is provide the structures, backgrounds and methodologies that will help the students of the introduction course to International Studies to understand global events and the role of people in it. It is then up to the instructor to connect the lectures to current events, and up to the students to keep track of daily events.

The term 'global' is not without contestation. Many scholars will argue that it denies the particularities of the local and the individual. That is a valid concern. But at the same time, we cannot deny that certain developments happening across the world share distinct similarities and therefore merit the denomination 'global'. International Studies as conceived in this textbook seeks to connect the dimensions of the global and the individual. To do so, this textbook will use a framework of globalism (consisting of 'global structures', 'global trends' and 'global challenges') that are superimposed on the dimensions of the local, national and global, and viewed from a perspective of human and social sciences. This structure will be elaborated further in the following chapters.

The notion of 'International Studies' is in its infancy and has not yet been fully conceptualized. This textbook can therefore not be conclusive nor comprehensive, but it will contribute to the theorization of International Studies by offering a lay of the land and providing International Studies students with concepts, frameworks and viewpoints to navigate it. In doing so, it will make use of the ten years of experience we have built at the International Studies program of Leiden University. One of the pitfalls I learned to avoid during these years, is the geographical and epistemological vantage points that come with teaching at a university in Western

Europe. Currently, International Studies are predominantly taught at universities in Europe and North America which is why this textbook provides frameworks and concepts that are relevant to the wide variety of societies and experiences of the entire world, not just the Western world.

PART I

What is International Studies?

The aim of International Studies is to understand the global complexities of the world in which we live by means of the role that people play in these complexities. International Studies has the character of a 3-D chessboard due to the interaction of local, regional, and global dimensions. This interaction is the focal point of study with the human individual as the main driver. In addition to these approaches, this textbook introduces three global scopes that will help the student of International Studies understand and analyze the 'global complexities': global structures, global trends and global challenges. These scopes will provide the framework of this textbook, whereby each scope will be elaborated in several thematic chapters.

This textbook approaches International Studies as a field of study that will enable students to navigate the three dimensions and the complexity of global issues. Rather than being a specialist in any academic field, International Studies students will be given a broad overview of the various fields and disciplines and therefore the ability to look beyond traditional academic boundaries. To accomplish this, this textbook offers five interconnected approaches to International Studies: interaction of the local and the global; the human perspective; the contemporary perspective; inter- and multidisciplinarity; and diversity. Each approach will be discussed separately in the chapters below.

> A **global event** is any situation that has global repercussions, like a tsunami that hits numerous coastal areas, or a war that causes massive migration. A **global complexity** is one or a series of global events that create a complex social or political situation on a global scale, like the Ukraine-Russia war that has caused a large stream of refugees, impacted international grain supply, and stirred global political alliances.

CHAPTER 1

First perspective: interaction of the local and the global

The first perspective we consider in International Studies is the ability of the local to become global, and vice versa, and the interaction of the two. This may sound self-evident, but is very complex from an academic perspective because it demands continuously zooming in and out. The following notions will help navigate these multiple dimensions.

3-D chessboard

In International Relations, it is now recognized that domestic and global policies are interconnected (also known as 'intermestics'), and that studying them separately or, worse, focusing on one while neglecting the other, does not contribute to a full understanding of the situation under study. International Studies as conceived in this textbook, translates this notion of intermestics into three spatial dimensions not unlike a 3-D chessboard. These dimensions are **the local, the national and the global**. The local can range from the level of the individual to that of an organisation or or a town, the national refers to states and the global to everything that surpasses the state (like international organizations and corporations). In the second half of the 20th century, the national and global dimensions also started merging into a hybrid form called region, and 'regionalism' has become the name for states who endeavor to create spheres of shared economy, politics or culture.

In between and intersecting with these three dimensions are numerous other actors at play, like international corporations, transnational communities, criminal organizations and religious institutions. Yet in the middle of all of them is the **human individual**, because it is only human individuals who can set any of these dimensions into motion.

> **Intermestics** is a term used in International Relations to denote the inter-connectedness between domestic and international policies.

The interaction of these **three dimensions** is the field of study of International Studies. For instance, local events may spark national uprisings that, in turn, can resonate on a global level. The Tunisian salesman who set himself on fire in 2011 in response to police abuse, triggered a national uprising that set in motion a series of revolts across the Arab world. Or the highly infectious Covid virus that erupted in China and quickly spread across borders, growing into a worldwide pandemic. Likewise, national events can have global as well as local repercussions elsewhere in the world. The 2023 actions of the Israeli army in Gaza not only caused friction among states globally but also within states across the world. Global events can also have both national and local effects, such as climate change, or a political-military divide like the Cold War, or an international human rights treaty.

With the emergence of communication technology, these three dimensions have acquired a virtual parallel: contacts made among people on any of the three levels can now also be made without these people physically meeting. While this may speed up the communication and information flows, it is also cause for concern. Can people handle that much information? Can people function socially when they do not meet physically? What is the effect of all this on the cohesion of societies, the performance on the work floor, the governance of a corporation or a country? These and other questions have become pertinent after the Covid-19 pandemic (2019-2022) and still need answers.

> The **3 dimensions** stand for three spatial dimensions: local, national and global. These dimensions, in their interconnectedness, are the domains in which human action takes place. In addition to the **physical** interaction among people in any of these dimensions, there also is an increasing **virtual** interaction by means of the multiple forms of communication.

Whatever global events or complexities are studied by students of International Studies, they require students to realize that the spatial dimensions play a role, and that the students should be able to move back and forth from one to the other to understand the issue at hand.

Two processes

On the 3-D chessboard of International Studies, we can discern two processes of interaction: globalization and glocalization.

Globalization
While the term *global* is an adjective that describes the nature of an event, *globalization* is a noun that refers to a process. Globalization means that the world has become **interconnected**: countries cooperate on a worldwide scale, large corporations do business across the world, international human rights organizations

are campaigning in multiple countries, disasters and wars are immediately visible to everyone on social media, and pandemics move across borders faster than ever before. It must be noted that globalization can have two meanings: it may refer to the political, social, economic or other human processes that have become globalized, but it may also refer to the policies that governments have put in play that, in turn, have set such processes in motion. In this textbook, globalization refers to the processes.

Because of this interconnectedness, local events can have global repercussions, and vice versa. In 2005, for instance, a cartoon in a small local Danish newspaper about the prophet Mohammed led to demonstrations all over the Muslim world and created global tensions between the Western and Muslim world. Similarly, the arrest and subsequent death of an Afro-American man in the United States in May 2020 spurred the Black Lives Matter movement that led to protests all over the Western world.

Being interconnected oftentimes creates **interdependence**: an action by one of the stakeholders of a global network can have repercussions for the entire network. The worldwide economic crisis of 2008 started with the popping of a financial bubble in the American housing market, and this led to a financial crisis on a global scale because the worldwide financial sector had become interdependent. Likewise, the 2019 Covid-19 pandemic started in China but quickly spread due to the globalized and very dynamic transport networks. To stop the pandemic, these networks had to be shut down, which had enormous implications worldwide on a social and on an economic level.

> **Globalization** means that states, organizations, and people are interconnected on a worldwide scale.

> The terms '**international**' and '**global**' are often used interchangeably. However, there is a slight difference: 'international' usually refers to states or regions; 'global' denotes an interconnectedness on a world scale that can be among a variety of actors.

Glocalization

So far, we have discussed how local issues can have global consequences. When it happens the other way round, so when global events have local consequences or local expressions, it is called glocalization. For instance, the idea of socialism gained worldwide popularity in the early twentieth century, and became a truly global ideology, but was adapted to local tastes and circumstances: the socialism of the Soviet Union was different from that in China, and the socialist leader Nkrumah of Ghana had different ideas from his colleagues in Asia and South America, just like the socialists in northern European countries had their own interpretation of socialism. Of a completely different order is rap music, which is another example of glocalization: it has taken the world by storm, but the fact that it is performed in the local language and deals with local issues makes that this global phenomenon has become very localized. The interaction of globalization and glocalization takes place on numerous levels. If we visualize a network spanning the world, we can imagine all kinds of goods, information and ideas circling the world at dazzling speed, being uploaded, so to speak, into the global networks of communication and transported, downloaded everywhere in the world.

> **Glocalization** is when global events or phenomena have local consequences or local expressions.

Three scopes

In addition to the 3-D chessboard with its two processes of globalization and glocalization, this textbook introduces three different scopes through which we can view these dynamics: structures, trends, and challenges.

Global structures
When people are active on a local or national level, they are often confronted with structures or mechanisms that exist everywhere, and that have become pervasive in human interactions. In this textbook we call these global structures. At some point in time, they were created by humankind and they are characterized by a certain degree of permanence and pervasiveness.

There are two kinds of global structures. Some are almost as old as humankind, like belief systems, the patriarchy, the arts, the economy, war and peace, migration. These structures may take very different forms (belief systems exist as mythologies, religions, ideologies; economies can be based on barter or on money, or they may be aimed at the redistribution of wealth or at the protection of private property), but their essence remains the same. In many instances, that essence has evolved into a variety of traditions. The other kind of global structures is what people have developed at various points in history and which have since become engrained and permanent across the world. Examples include the nation-state, international organizations, international law and diplomacy.

The process of globalization may enhance but also disrupt established global structures. An example of such disruption is the ancient global structure of diplomacy, whereby rulers and governments communicate with each other through ambassadors. In modern times, until half a century ago, everything international was handled by national Ministries of Foreign Affairs and their international networks of embassies. Museums or companies that wanted to establish relationships with colleagues abroad would solicit the help of their embassies. But because of globalization, that is often no longer the case. Large companies don't bother with diplomats but establish their own international contacts. And directors of museums or mayors of large cities may not ask permission or advice from their Ministry of Foreign affairs but establish their own relations with cities and museums abroad.

> A **global structure** is a mechanism or organization that is globally embedded in human interactions and is the result of cooperation or tradition. A global structure is always human made. See Part 2 for further discussion.

Global trends

What is referred to in this textbook as a global trend is when a manner of thinking or behaving gains worldwide recognition or emulation. An example is nationalism: it emerged in the nineteenth century and quickly enveloped the entire world. Nationalism 'caught on' globally and had enormous repercussions locally. Other examples of such trends are modernization and secularization in the first half of the twentieth century, religionization since the 1970s, securitization since the 2000s. The reason and timing of global trends is often unclear. We can merely observe that such trends happen and greatly influence people's thinking and actions worldwide.

The difference between a global trend and a global structure is that a global trend is not yet fully embedded in human interactions. Some global trends may gradually evolve into global structures (like the nation-state), but some trends may also lose their traction and dissolve (for instance, it is argued that the global trend of international cooperation that started in late 1940s is on the decline). Some global trends transformed in unexpected ways. It was believed, for instance, that the modernity of the twentieth century, with its emphasis on rationalism and science, would push religion to the background or even make it obsolete. It did not: religion became a factor of social and political significance from the 1970s onwards. Similarly, it was believed that national and international solidarity would make nationalism disappear. It did not: in the second half of the twentieth century, nationalism started to re-emerge with a force that took everyone by surprise.

In International Studies it is important to recognize global trends because they may explain much of what is happening in a certain period. Nationalism, for example, was an incentive in the nineteenth and early twentieth centuries to think about a society as a single people that shared the same language, history and religion. This led to many cases of ethnic and religious cleansing and contributed to the high number of states in the twentieth century. The study of today's global trends is a challenge however, because it is hard to recognize them: people usually consider the times they live in as 'normal' and not as part of an upcoming or passing trend, and even when people do realize something is happening that helps define their time (as was the case with populism in the 1990s, or with the decline of multilateralism in the 2020s) it's often difficult to identify exactly what it is and how it affects the world.

> A **global trend** is a manner of thinking or behaving that gains worldwide recognition or is emulated globally. Global trends happen at moments and in ways that are usually unforeseen. See Part 3 for further discussion.

Global challenge

A global challenge is a problematic issue on a global scale that affects people worldwide, and that needs to be addressed by the concerted efforts of various actors on an international scale. Examples include climate change, migration, 'policing' of international peace and justice, and sustainable development. These global complexities cannot be solved on a national level: international cooperation is needed to address them.

An interesting aspect about global challenges is that they usually only gain that status once they are recognized as such. There is, in other words, a difference between the *existence* of a global challenge and the *recognition* of one. For instance, scientists and policymakers have been warning against climate change since the 1970s, but it only became a global challenge when it was put on the international agenda in the early 2000s. Another example is terrorism: nationalist and left-wing terrorism existed around the world in the 1970s, and Muslim militants were a menace in the Arab world during the 1990s, but it was only considered a global threat after the 9/11 attacks in 2001 against Americans on American soil and after subsequent attacks in Europe. Conversely, policymakers may also decide *not* to allow a problematic global issue to turn into a global challenge. This has been the case with the Covid-19 pandemic, when the presidents of the United States, Brazil and Belarus tried to downplay the gravity of the corona pandemic, refusing to consider it an issue of national emergency, let alone something that needed an international approach.

> A **global challenge** is a problematic issue on a global scale that affects people worldwide, and that needs to be addressed by the concerted efforts of various actors. A global issue becomes a global challenge once it is recognized as such. See Part 4 for further discussion

Some examples of interacting and overlapping global structures, trends, challenges

Migration: People have been migrating for as long as they have been inhabiting the earth. As such migration is a global structure. But many of today's migrations – especially of refugees and illegal migrant workers – are also designated as global challenges, and to address them, global structures like international treaties on refugees and the International Organization for Migration are called upon.

Democracy: while democracy has a long history and manifests itself in many ways, it became a truly global trend in the 1990s: democratic reforms took place in many Asian, African and South American countries, and people took to the streets in countries like China, Mongolia and most eastern European countries calling for government reforms that would lead to democracy. Demonstrations like these would recur in the decades after that, ranging from the Color Revolutions in Ukraine, Georgia and Kyrgyzstan to the Arab Spring in 2011 and the uprisings of 2019 in Hong Kong, the Middle East and South America. These events showed the glocalization of democracy in the many different ways that countries view and structure their democracy. And whereas most Western countries saw this global trend as the start of a better and more liberal era that should ideally turn into a global structure, states like Russia and China considered these developments a global challenge.

Pandemics: Pandemics are a recurring phenomenon in the history of mankind (think of the plague or the Spanish flu). Recent pandemics, like the Mexican flu (2009) and Ebola (2014) were treated as local problems. Covid-19 in 2019 was at first also considered a local issue (China), but once it started to spread it became clear that concerted efforts were needed worldwide to fight this disease: Covid-19 became a global challenge. Some global structures were severely affected by it, like the global economy, while other global structures, like the World Health Organization, geared up to confront it. The glocalization of the pandemic showed in the different manners in which it was handled in each country.

Climate change: In 1972, the Club of Rome, a think tank of intellectuals and business leaders, published *The Limits to Growth*, a study on the problems the planet was facing due to excessive production and consumption. This was one of the first warning signs for the global challenge of climate change. But it took until the 2000s for climate change not to be an issue of discussion but a generally accepted scientific fact, and as such also an accepted global challenge. Global structures like the United Nations are at the forefront of addressing this challenge.

Further reading

Arjun Appadurai (ed.), *Globalization*, Durham & London, 2001

Scott Lash and Roland Robertson (eds.), *Global Modernities*, Sage 1995

George Ritzer (ed.), *The Blackwell Companion to Globalization*, Blackwell Publishing, 2007

Saskia Sassen, 'Globalization or Denationalization?' *Review of International Political Economy*, Vol.10, No.1, 2003, pp. 1-22

Joseph E. Stiglitz, 'The overselling of globalization', *Business Economics*, Vol.52, No.3, 2017, pp. 129-137

Second perspective: people

International issues are commonly studied by an academic discipline called International Relations. Their focus is on international politics and economics, and therefore predominantly on the ways states interact. However, in International Studies the dominant focus is on the role of people. This domain of academic study is reserved for Social Sciences and Humanities. But whereas these disciplines usually focus on individuals and communities in their local environment, International Studies explores the role of these people in a global context. This textbook provides the following concepts that will help the student of International Studies understand the interaction between the individual and the global world.

Agency

In International Studies, the dominant focus is on the role of people – as persons, from the individual worker or parent to religious or national leaders – but also on their ideas and cultures, on their organized forms as communities and, in a final stage, on the roles they play in states and international organizations. These are the mentioned three dimensions of the local, the national and the global. A key notion when studying the role of the individual in these three dimensions is **agency**, which refers to the power and potential of individuals to shape their own lives. This does not mean that people are the determining factor in what is happening in their lives. Much happens that is outside of their control. The question is then how they will respond which effectively is also a form of agency.

The notion of agency challenges the traditional approach of studying states and (usually male) leaders by contending that *all* people play a role. Studies have subsequently been directed at uncovering the voices and roles of women, people of color, the enslaved, and people of lower socio-economic classes. The notion of agency allows students of International Studies to get a much wider view of the actors who play a role in the global complexities of this world.

Agency refers to the power and potential of each individual to shape their own life.

While agency is a useful concept for studying individuals, some academic challenges remain. One such challenge is how to study the needs and desires of individuals when considering that these individuals interact with each other. Are the needs and desires really those of the individuals who express them or are they influenced by or copied from peer groups (family, friends, communities)? Or are these needs and desires perhaps an intricate part of the political, economic and social dynamics that play on a national and global scale? In the social sciences this dilemma is also known as the '**structure-agency duality**', which explores the balance between free will of the individual and the constraints or other influences of their environment. The assumption is that social structures such as social class, religion, gender, ethnicity, family and culture, but also political structures like laws, bureaucracies, governments and states may limit (or motivate!) individuals to exercise their agency. Studying these processes will help students of International Studies understand the dynamics of global events.

> The **structure-agency duality** explores the balance between the agency of the individual and the constraints or influences of their environment.

Another challenge when exploring the concept of agency is how this may affect others. The focus of agency is usually on the individual's needs, desires, drives and capacities. Agency studied in this manner may then explain much about people's individual behavior, but not how that agency interacts with local, national or global issues. When researching the impact that people may have on others and how they may set something in motion that may or may not have a global impact, the Social Sciences often use the notion of the **change agent**. This is a notion that has been applied in a wide variety of contexts, ranging from the mass communicator and educator to human rights activists. Oftentimes the term change agent is used in combination with the concept of leadership, but the two are not necessarily the same. Consider, for example, a group of people who want to protest against something, so they post a time and place for this protest on social media, and several hundred people show up. Some people present made the first move in this scenario and may be considered change agents, but there is no act of leadership.

> A **change agent** is someone who advocates or causes change in an organization or society. The notion of change agent is often used in conjunction with – but is not always the same as – the notion of **leadership**.

3-I's

Agency considers the actions of people, but another important question is what motivates people in today's global setting: what makes them tick? The answer to this question is of course immensely complex but can, for the sake of simplicity, be reduced to what this textbook refers to as the **3-I's: interests, ideas, identities**. Examples of people's basic **interests** include safety, food, water, health, and access to resources (whereby the needed resources may change over time: for instance, lithium as a raw material for electrical batteries has recently become of primal importance). The second 'I' is that of **ideas**, which encompass ideologies and religions, whereby the belief in these ideas is a powerful motivator. The third 'I' stands for **identities**, which has multiple components, such as language, culture, customs and histories.

> The **3-I's** stand for **interests, ideas, identities**. They represent the basic motivators for people's behaviors and thoughts.

The 3-I's play a role in all global events and complexities of today. Sometimes because people are the cause of such events. If they are, the 3-I's are at the root of people's *actions*. Certain ideas may be the cause for war, for instance, just like the pursuit of certain interests may lead to the establishment of large corporations and the development of technologies, or to economic meltdowns and the depletion of resources. In other instances, people may need to *respond* to regional or global events like a pandemic, climate change or migration, and are forced to make choices and take decisions which are always driven by their interests, ideas or identities. For instance, migration can be welcomed out of economic interest or feared as a negative impact on a society's identity. Covid-19 was believed by some to be a mere flu, by others to be a public health hazard, and by yet others to be a government conspiracy to gain more power. These perceptions are decisive for how that global event is dealt with: it can make quite a difference if an issue is considered an economic opportunity, a political challenge or a social problem. Sometimes perceptions are so widely shared that they have a global impact (a process that has accelerated exponentially with the emergence of social media). After Covid-19, for instance, it appears that the mistrust of vaccinations became a global trend.

Humanities

As mentioned, the main disciplines involved in studying International Studies are Humanities and Social Sciences. Many universities distinguish between the two: 'Humanities' are all disciplines that study the thoughts of people and their expression thereof (like history, languages, theology, philosophy, arts) while 'Social Sciences' are all disciplines that study the behavior of people (like anthropology, psychology, sociology, political sciences). In this textbook, however, we are joining all these subjects together under the heading 'Humanities' as the study of the behavior and thoughts of people. Furthermore, as we will see in the next chapters, Law and Economics, although often treated as disciplines separate from Humanities, also play distinctive roles in International Studies.

Humanities in this textbook is the study of the behaviour and thoughts of people.

Academic studies are traditionally divided into Humanities and Natural Sciences (which deal with the material world, like flora and fauna, planets and stars, living organisms and lifeless materials). A distinct difference between the two categories is that the Natural Sciences have the possibility of conducting accurate measurements through which they can prove or disprove hypotheses. That is also why they are called the exact sciences. The Humanities, on the other hand, have a much more elusive research object: humankind. And humans have a few characteristics that can make accurate measurement challenging.

First, humans appear to be rather unpredictable. For instance, the large political events in recent decades that had a global impact, like the Iranian Revolution in 1979, the fall of the Berlin wall in 1989 and the Arab Spring in 2011 were not predicted by the hundreds of experts that were monitoring these areas. Contrary to the Natural Sciences, humans, it seems, are not governed by laws that, once we understand them, can be used to predict what people will do.

Second, while both humans and animals are motivated by *interests* – survival, food, resources – humans are typically also motivated by *ideas* and *identities*. Revolutions have been started because of ideas, wars because of national identities. The Americans rose in revolt spurred on by a piece of paper that started with 'We, the people', and the Belgian revolt of independence was sparked by an opera. The many calls for freedom or independence are more than a claim of rights, just like a demonstration for peace is more than an appeal to principles. Often there are underlying driving forces of human emotions like hope, despair, fear, pride. These are human qualities that are not always easy to put in a simple academic equation. The same applies to the many forms of communication that humankind has at its disposal like language, arts, music. Speeches are known for having roused entire populations, giving them a sense of unity and purpose. Similarly, music is one of those typical human abilities that can wield enormous power: there are plenty of examples of songs that unite and empower people, whether during religious gatherings, rock concerts or revolutions.

The third characteristic that distinguishes the Natural Sciences from Humanities is that students of Humanities are humans themselves. Studying one's own species poses certain academic problems. Can students of Humanities, being humans themselves, be sufficiently objective and neutral in the pursuit of these studies? This question challenges the academic quality and integrity of study. Some scholars hold an **absolutist** view by claiming that Humanities are just another science, and they practice the study of Humanities with empirical research based on evidence and hard truths. Others hold a **relativist** view: they argue that the subjectivity of the researcher cannot be denied or neutralized and must therefore be taken into account when conducting research (see also chapter 'Diversity').

The relativist viewpoint gained momentum with the theory of **Postmodernism** which argues that reality and morality are not set in stone but are human constructs. According to postmodernists, since there are no laws of nature that determine how humankind works, and one can never prove that God or the universe has set rules that determine what is right or wrong, there remain only the rules set by humans themselves. In other words, according to this viewpoint, people shape their own way of looking at the world. Postmodernism, therefore, is against lending permanence and authority to knowledge and values. While this reasoning has a certain logic, it also risks making any kind of research into humankind almost impossible.

Further reading

Margaret Archer, 'Structure, Culture and Agency', in Mark D. Jacobs and Nancy Weiss Hanrahan (eds.), *The Blackwell Companion to the Sociology of Culture*, Blackwell Publishing, 2005, pp.17-34

Chatterjee, I., Kunwar, J., & Frank den Hond, 'Anthony Giddens and structuration theory,' in S. Clegg, & M. Pina e Cunha (Eds.), *Management, Organizations and Contemporary Social Theory*, Routledge, 2019, pp. 60-79

Matt Holland, 'The Change Agent', in: Bruce J Reid and W. Foster (eds.), *Achieving cultural change in networked libraries*, Aldershot: Gower, 2000, pp.105-107

M. Schlosser, 'Agency', *Stanford Encyclopedia of Philosophy*, 2019 (rev.)

Susan P. Shapiro, 'Agency Theory', *Annual Review of Sociology*, Vol. 31, 2005) pp. 263-284

Sherman Tan, 'Understanding the "Structure" and "Agency" Debate in the Social Sciences,' in Kathleen Powers (ed.), *Habitus. Vol1: The Forum*, 36-50

CHAPTER 3

Third perspective: the contemporary

International Studies as presented in this textbook regard the world from the perspective of the here and now. We do not work our way from the past to the present, but we start with the present and look at the past only if it can help us understand the present. There are two reasons for this approach.

The focus on today

The first reason to take the perspective of the here and now is simply that our present world and its current events are what we engage with every day. In International Studies we want to make sense of the world around us as it is now. But to study this contemporary world in an academic fashion is not easy. We are too involved, too close, it's happening now and so we have little time for distance or reflection. That goes against the nature of most scholars who want to be able to take a step back and take time to study and consider. But students of International Studies are often confronted with issues that are playing out in real life, right now. International Studies as expounded in this textbook aims to train students to use a broad knowledge combined with a set of analytical tools from various disciplines to evaluate the world around us as it is evolving today.

Recent global changes

The second reason to take a contemporary perspective is that our world has undergone some unprecedented global changes in the past decades that affect us here and now. Perhaps the most significant one is demographics: the world population has doubled since 1970. This has an impact on the world's resources, food production and climate. Another unprecedented phenomenon is the enormous increase in literacy worldwide. This means that more people than ever before have access to information. With the advancements of social media technology since the turn of the millennium, this access has grown to global proportions.

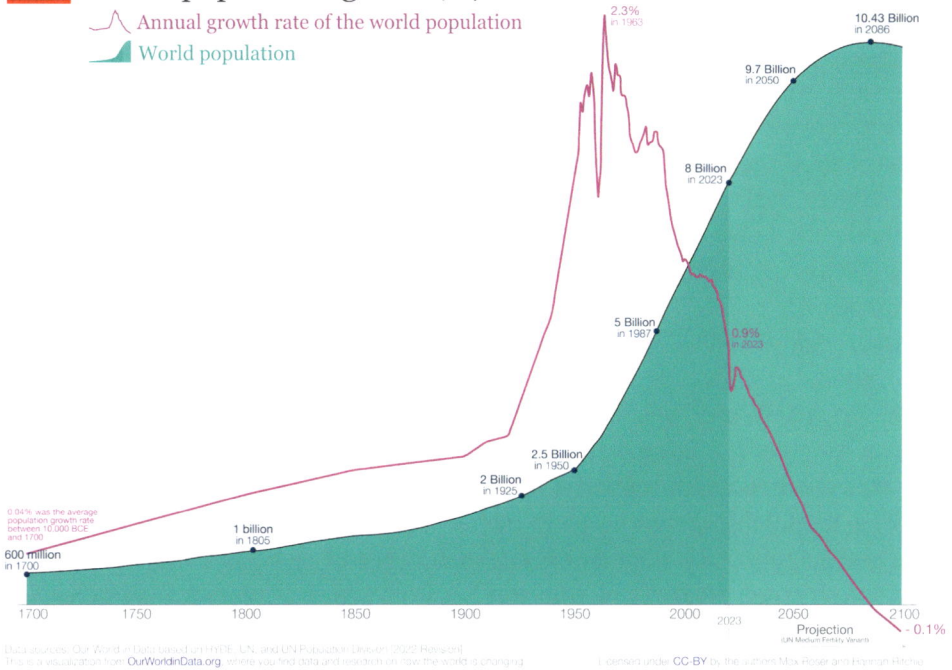

Figure I.3.1 World population growth

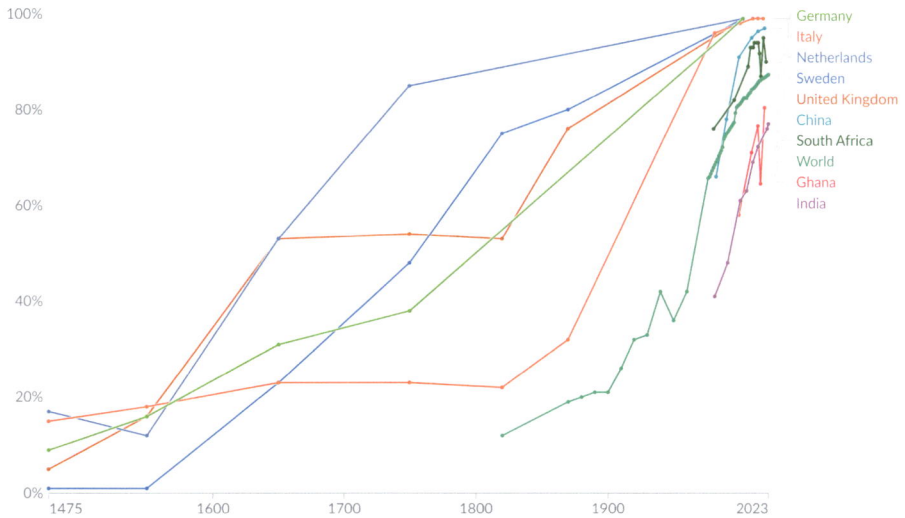

Figure I.3.2 Literacy rate

Another factor of considerable change in the recent past is the increase of the number of actors on the world stage: in addition to a rising number of states (the number of UN member states has almost quadrupled since 1948), there is also an increasing number of non-state actors that play a role in international and global politics: international corporations (like Shell or Procter & Gamble), humanitarian and ecological organizations (like Amnesty International, Greenpeace and Oxfam), international economic organizations (like the IMF and World Bank), but also criminal and militant organizations. All these developments have contributed to an increase in encounters between local, national and global levels – in short: globalization.

Also, many new *global structures* have emerged over the past decades. International treaties, international bodies (like the International Organization for Migration, the World Health Organisation), regional cooperations (like ASEAN, African Union or the European Union), international financial systems – these are just a few examples of the mechanisms and organizations that operate on a regional or global level. Most are the result of intensive international cooperation.

A similar recent development is the emergence of new *global trends*. Until the twentieth century, the ordering principle between people in almost all societies was based on social standing, colour, gender or religion, structures which were gradually dismantled during the twentieth century. These traditional social classifications were replaced with the notion of equality – a concept that has a long history but that was arguably been put into full practice since the second half of the twentieth century. This has been a game changer (even if practicing genuine equality wasn't always successful, and is still work in progress), not only for national societies but also for the international community, as we will see in later chapters. Similarly, but in a much later stage, identity has become dominant in public and political discourse since the 2010s, with #MeToo and Black Lives Matters as prominent movements with a global impact.

Did these changes make our world a different world? That's not a question this textbook intends to answer. We merely observe that right now, the world is very much driven by recent global developments.

Crisis

Working on present issues often requires dealing with unexpected events. In the 1950s, when British prime minister Harold MacMillan was asked by a young journalist about the greatest challenge for a statesman, he famously answered "Events, dear boy, events." Unexpected events may sometimes take the form of what is called a 'crisis'. This has become a catch word in today's parlance: it usually refers to a problem that was not foreseen and that needs immediate attention. This, in turn, often means that ongoing matters are being put on hold and all resources and time are directed at solving that crisis. A crisis may require – or serve as an excuse for – solutions that break with existing tradition, law or bureaucracy. Whether these solutions are beneficial or detrimental to a society or its people depends on how you look at it: for instance, an administrative crisis may lead to an overhaul of an institution to make it more effective, an economic crisis may prompt a restructuring that affects people's jobs, and a social crisis is usually the pretext for revolutionaries or the military to start a revolution or stage a coup. Since the early 2000s, the characterization of an event as a 'crisis' is often done in terms of security, which has its own dynamics (see chapter 'Security').

'Crisis'

"In all the human and social sciences, crisis appears as a key concept; in history, of course, to characterize epochs or structures. Political science tries to operationalize the term and distinguish it from 'conflict'. (...) 'Crisis' is often used interchangeably with 'unrest,' 'conflict,' 'revolution,' and to describe vaguely disturbing moods or situations. (...) The concept of crisis, which once had the power to pose unavoidable, harsh and non-negotiable alternatives, has been transformed to fit the uncertainties of whatever might be favored at a given moment."

(Kosseleck Reinhart and Michaela Richter, 'Crisis', *Journal of the History of Ideas*, 2006)

The past and the future

This emphasis on current events may give the false impression that the past is not relevant. To the contrary. The past is of crucial importance to understand the present: how did we get here? That sounds like a simple history lesson, but it isn't. There are different ways to look at the past. For instance, do we believe that humankind improves as we move forward in time (which is often implied by the term 'progress')? And is the sequence of events that we call history a series of events that logically follow one after another, with a subsequent series of causes and effects, or is it all random? And to what extent is history colored by people's identity, their culture or their ideas about society or politics? These questions are of great relevance to students of International Studies.

To understand the present, we need to appreciate how the roads taken in the past have brought us to where we are today. This is called **process tracing** which is the analysis of all the elements that may have led to a certain event. This may sound very straightforward, but the analysis itself as well as its underlying assumptions can be quite complex because of their human dimensions. Were these roads leading up to significant events taken deliberately or randomly, were decision makers consciously choosing war or merely sleepwalking into it, were people driven by material interests (land, resources, power) or by emotional or cultural considerations (honour, anger, revenge)? And, perhaps most importantly, can the road taken ever be un-taken, in other words, is reversal of actions possible?

> **Process tracing** is the analysis of all the elements (historical, cultural, political, religious, etc.) that may have led to a certain event. Important questions in this analysis are **when** (when did events take place, in what order), **what** (what are the constituent elements of this process, what are the dynamics at play), **why** (why are the elements of this process relevant, and why did they happen in the sequence they did) and **how** (how did the combination of all these elements lead to the event under study).

While the roads taken have led us to today, we make choices today that have an impact on our **futures**. Today, therefore, acts as a linchpin between the past and the future. And while many leaders try to make decisions that are aimed at the future – agreements on climate change, wars to eradicate terrorism, economic policies to alleviate poverty – many of these decisions are also prompted by the urges of today: we want a better life, we want a better world, or we simply want more. And we want it now. Thinking about the future therefore requires some effort to look beyond the present. In doing so, we can distinguish two ways of thinking about the future. One way tries to predict what may happen in the future. This type of thinking about the future tries to answer the question 'What can we expect?' by extrapolating existing data into the future. Examples are the future of Middle Eastern politics, world economics, the state of technology in fifty years. The other way of thinking about the future explores new possibilities which previously seemed unthinkable by asking the question 'Where do we want to be in the future?'. Contrary to the intellectual exercise of prediction, this requires thinking outside the box. This may lead to scenario-based thinking, but can also express itself through arts, literature and other non-academic pursuits. Change agents are typically people who take leaps forward by imagining something that to many seemed unimaginable.

> **Future thinking: prediction and imagination**
> **Prediction** answers the question 'What can we expect?' by extrapolating existing data into the future. Examples are the future of the politics in the Middle East, the economy in the world, the state of technology in fifty years. **Imagination** asks the question 'Where do we want to be in the future?' and explores new possibilities which previously seemed unthinkable.

Researching today's issues

One of the challenges faced by students of International Studies researching a situation that is taking place today – apart from the choice of methods and theories (see next chapter 'Multi- and inter-disciplinarity) – is the choice of research data. Academic research commonly makes use of either primary sources (field work, court rulings, policy documents, original writings, etc.) or secondary sources. Secondary sources are required to be academically sound, which usually means that they must be peer-reviewed. The process of research, peer-reviewing, and publishing is time consuming which means that at best, secondary academic literature is usually only available two or three years after the event. Students who want to research events or situations that are happening 'now' are therefore faced with the problem of finding sufficient literature on the subject. One option is to use reports produced by international organizations, research institutions and think tanks. These often make use of scientific methods to collect data, but their reports are not always academically sound because they may be selective or even biased in the collection and presentation of their data. It is therefore advised to take into account two factors when using such reports.

First, students should assess the 'color' of the institution that has produced the report: who are its financiers and what are its aims? Is the institution established to promote certain political or commercial viewpoints, or is its aim merely to collect certain data? And are the institution's reports valued by other researchers? The outcome of such preliminary research does not necessarily have to disqualify that organization, but it should make students more alert to possible flaws in the information provided. One way to deal with such reliability issues is to make a cross-section of several reports on the same topic and either come to a weighted average of the information or acknowledge that the information is still inconclusive.`

The second factor to consider is that the student discards any opinion or advocacy that such reports may contain and only uses the facts and data that they provide. This will require the student to make an assessment on the way that these data have been collected. If this data appears to be haphazard or based on hearsay or on local newspapers, then it might be best not to use it. Information provided by autocratic states should also be handled with suspicion. However, the data in such reports is often provided by local actors, such as human rights organizations. But whatever the source of information, it is up to the student to make a critical evaluation of it. Once the useful data is distilled from the – preferably more than one – report, the student should use academic methods and theories (see next chapter) to make an analysis of these data. Existing secondary academic literature on similar cases may also prove useful as a matter of comparison.

Further reading

Hannah Arendt, *Between Past and Future*, The Viking Press, 1961

Andrew Bennett and Jeffrey T. Checkel, *Process Tracing. From Metaphor to analytical Tool*, Cambridge University Press, 2014

Sarah Cooper, *Making History Mine*, Routledge, 2009

Sarah Maza, *Thinking about History*, University of Chicago Press, 2017

John Rennie Short, *Global Dimensions. Space, Place and the Contemporary World*, Reaktion Books, 2001

Taryne Jade Taylor, Isiah Lavender III, Grace L. Dillon, and Bodhisattva Chattopadhyay (eds.), *The Routledge Handbook of CoFuturisms*, Routledge, 2024

Fourth perspective: multi- and interdisciplinarity

In the previous chapters we have seen that the student of International Studies must learn to navigate the 3-D chessboard of the local, the national and the global. Traditionally, these three dimensions are also represented by different academic disciplines: Anthropology to study the local, Sociology and Political Science to study the national, International Relations to study the global. To this we may add the multiple disciplines that are represented by the 3-I's: *Interests* are studied by disciplines like Economics and Political Science; *Ideas* by Religious Studies, Philosophy, Arts and Literature, Law, History; *Identity* by Cultural Anthropology, Linguistics, Area Studies. How to navigate this multitude of disciplinary approaches?

Multi- and inter-disciplinarity

Academic disciplines tend to highlight a particular angle of a situation. For instance, people may fight each other because of a lack of resources (that is a typical economical perspective), or because they dislike each other (that would interest anthropologists), because the other has customs that are considered blasphemous (Religious Studies), because the other is breaking rules (that's how lawyers look at it) or because leaders have whipped up their people with inflammatory rhetoric (Communication Studies and Linguistics). International Studies wants to provide a framework of study that enables the student to use as many academic perspectives as are needed to understand a particular global complexity. Ideally speaking, the perspectives of as many different disciplines as possible should be represented in the study of this one topic, but even the combination of two or three disciplines will already yield more and newer insights than the use of a single discipline.

Combining two or more disciplines is called the **multidisciplinary** approach. This is beneficial to reaching a better understanding of the issue at hand, but it also poses a challenge to the student because it adds to the already complex 3-D chessboard that is International Studies. Not only does one need to zoom in an out from the individual to the global level and back, and to move from one place on the globe to another; one also may have to switch from one academic discipline to another. The academic scholar specialized in one discipline will scoff at this approach: it is too much and will therefore harm the quality and detail of the research. That may be true. But what the International Studies student will be able to do that the specialist cannot, is to connect the dots across various geographical and disciplinary areas, which may result in a better understanding of global complexities than a mono-disciplinary specialist will be able to assess.

Another approach that some scholars advocate is to take the elements of various disciplines and merge them in a new, coherent framework that is tailor-made for the study of the issue at hand. This is known as the **interdisciplinary** approach. This requires a high degree of knowledge of the academic disciplines that one intends to synthesize. Most researchers, however, remain in their mono-disciplinary field, and if they venture into multidisciplinary research, they usually do so by cooperating with colleagues of different disciplines to jointly study the issue at hand, each from their own disciplinary angle.

> **Multi-disciplinarity** is the use of more than one discipline to understand the issue at hand. **Inter-disciplinarity** is the mixing of more than one discipline, thereby creating hybrid disciplines that provide new perspectives on the issue at hand. Since disciplines have become specialized fields of study, each with its own terminology and methodologies, it is relatively easier to use a multi-disciplinary approach (which only requires that the student has mastered the selected disciplines or cooperates with those who have mastered them) than to create a new and academically sound interdisciplinary approach.

Theory and methodology

Every discipline in Humanities has developed its own set of methodologies and theories. A **theory** offers an explanation of what we observe. Theories do not represent truths but provide ways of understanding. Neither are theories scientific laws that accurately describe, determine and predict how things work. The more accurate a theory is in explaining events, and the wider the range of situations that the theory can be applied to, the more valid it will be considered.

Different disciplines may ask different questions and therefore develop different theories. For instance, if one is to study the demonstrations in Hong Kong against Chinese rule in 2019, does one look at it from a political, sociological, international, cultural, media, or other perspective? Framing theory can be helpful when taking the political perspective, social movement theory when taking a sociological perspective, Orientalism when taking the perspective of Western media coverage, post-colonialism when viewing the situation in the context of Hong Kong as a former British colony. Not all theories are valid to a particular case: it is up to the student to select the one that is most helpful in understanding the issue at hand.

Theories are explanations of what we observe. These explanations are not hard truths ('this is so') but offer degrees of plausibility ('this could be understood in that way'). A theory will be considered more valuable if it is a) simple in its premises, b) proven accurate in its use, and c) applicable to more than one situation.

A **methodology** describes the manner in which research is carried out. It first involves the selection of period, actors and data. For instance, in the case of the 2019 demonstrations in Hong Kong against Chinese rule, should we study the Chinese government or the Hong Kong demonstrators, or perhaps the international media, the local police force, the parents of the demonstrators or the Hong Kong media? And is the data for the research collected by means of interviewing the main stakeholders, or going through newspaper articles or court records, or cataloging graffiti and slogans, or checking posts on social media, or perhaps a combination of these? Once these determinations have been made, the student needs to select the appropriate academic method by which to collect and interpret this information. For instance, Literature Studies have methodologies to interpret and understand written texts and oral presentations, Anthropology has elaborated methodologies to collect information from people (by means of interviews, participating observation, autobiographical research, etc.), History focuses on primary sources that are the written and oral sources of the actors themselves. The main purpose of these methodologies is to build a research approach that leads to an understanding of the research topic that is comprehensive, balanced and unbiased and, most importantly, that leads to information that is verifiable – in other words, information that can be checked and would yield the same outcome if it were to be repeated by others.

In the course of working in various disciplines and with various theories and methodologies, the student of International Studies will also be confronted with various **epistemologies**. This stands for the systems and processes of knowledge that are typical to a particular religious, cultural or political environment that the student is studying. The Western academic environment, for instance, has its own epistemology which is based on a rational system of deductive reasoning, with a focus on the individual, and a division between the religious and the secular spheres. Confucian or Islamic epistemologies, to name two other examples, may use very different paradigms. For instance, the divine is an intricate part of Islamic thinking, and the collective is central to Confucian thinking. Different epistemologies may therefore give very different outlooks on the same topic of study.

Epistemology is the approach to knowledge and how to arrive at it. A particular religious, cultural, or political environment can have its own epistemology, each with its own foundations, methods, and truth validation.

The challenge for the student of International Studies is to find ways through the myriads of epistemologies, theories and methodologies. The student should bear in mind that methods and theories are tools that are meant to make research easy, not to complicate the student's life as a researcher. The standards set by academic disciplines may sometimes appear as straightjackets or restrictive molds, but they are merely guidelines to come to research results that are academically sound. At the same time, the student of International Studies should keep in mind that the goal is to understand the 3-D dynamics of the topic of study, which requires a broader view than most other fields of study require.

Further reading

Stanley R. Barrett, *Anthropology: A Student's Guide to Theory and Method*, University of Toronto Press, 2009

Willem B. Drees, *What are the Humanities for?*, Cambridge University Press, 2021

Jeffrey Thomas Nealon and Susan Searls Giroux, Chapters 1 ('Why Theory?'), 2 ('Author/ity'), 4 ('Subjectivity'), in: *The Theory Toolbox: Critical Concepts for the Humanities, Arts, and Social Sciences*, Rowman & Littlefield Publishers, 2012

Cathy Nutbrown and Peter Clough, *A Student's Guide to Methodology*, Sage Publications, 2012 (3rd edition)

Fifth perspective: diversity

This final perspective ties together the previous four perspectives because of the element that unites them all: the student. Whereas the previous perspectives were related to the world around the student, students of International Studies should also be aware of their own perspectives on that world. These perspectives can be part of the students' personalities and backgrounds, but also of their academic environment. Two examples may illustrate the latter: the international classroom and the Western context of instruction.

International classroom

International Studies often attract students from diverse backgrounds, creating an 'international classroom' where students are exposed to different experiences and circumstances. Exposure to such a variety of behaviors and views may act as an eye-opener to some students, while others may find that confronting or even offending. Teachers and students must find a way to deal with this. However, it may be better not to avoid such confrontations, because this diversity offers International Studies a unique learning environment that allows such conflicts to take place on a scale that is small and presumably safe.

Western context

At Western universities, International Studies is currently most probably taught in English, using academic literature in the English language, that in most cases is also produced at Western universities. The advantage of a single academic language is that it enables international communication. A disadvantage is that the richness of academic resources available in other languages may be lost. One way to prevent that may be for International Studies students to make use of their own languages, and to master any language of their region of interest.

   Another disadvantage of this situation is that the study of International Studies runs the risk of becoming Western-oriented. Indeed, Humanities scholarship at Western universities has in recent decades come under substantial criticism for two reasons. One is that Western scholarship has developed its own epistemology that may provide views of the world that are limited (because other epistemologies are neglected) or even skewed (because Western scholarship may be ill-placed to fully understand and appreciate certain non-Western ideas or behaviours).

The other criticism of Humanities scholarship at Western universities is that it may have biased tendencies towards the rest of the world. This bias, so the critics say, is the result of these Western academic institutions being rooted in colonial times. In those days, many Europeans saw themselves as the pinnacle of civilization and considered Western culture, religion and customs the measuring stick for how things should be, and everything that was different was spoken of in terms of primitive or backward. In the 1970s, it was Edward Said who drew attention to the fact that this nineteenth-century condescending and negative manner of looking at the 'Orient' had also permeated European media and literature and had not really dissipated since. This bias, which was also shown to be prevalent in scholars, became known as **Orientalism**, after the title of Said's book. The notion of Orientalism has since become a warning sign for Western scholars and much has been undertaken since to correct these views. Some critics have argued that this bias in attitude is not exclusive to Westerners; they coined the term 'Occidentalism' for prejudiced views that non-Western people may have of the West and how that may permeate their academic scholarship. However, most universities in the non-Western world are modelled on Western universities, with Western curricula, textbooks and theories that may very well continue to disseminate an Orientalist narrative (see chapter 'Postcolonialism').

> **Orientalism** originally denoted the essentialist approach to 'the Orient' as constituting immutable and stereotyped characteristics of Arab and Asian culture and traditions. Orientalism is also used in a more general way as the imbedded bias that Westerners may have towards other parts of the world, and that also has permeated the Western academic knowledge production. It has been argued that Orientalism is not an exclusive Western attitude since similar biases to 'others' exist in other parts of the world as well.

The above illustrates how the student of International Studies may be confronted with situations in the learning environment that pose academic challenges. To address these challenges, the student must be able to work with diversity. Two types of diversity will be discussed here.

Academic diversity

In past decades it has become clear that sound research in the domain of Humanities does not only depend on good analytical and methodological skills. When academics work on topics that involve numerous cultural, religious, racial and other dimensions, their personal disposition also becomes an important factor: does the topic sollicit affinity or aversion, or perhaps preconceived notions about it? Self-awareness of one's views, attitudes and background are therefore of paramount importance to conduct research that is academically sound. This is called **positionalit**y, a concept that requires every individual student to reflect on the manner in which they relate to the topic of research. Such reflection, however, is not an easy task when we realize that many of our preconceptions are so deeply embedded in our minds that we don't even consider them to be subjective.

The acknowledgement of one's positionality is no guarantee that we can undo it. Oftentimes we will be unable or unwilling to do so. For instance, gender equality is a non-negotiable given for some, while others will hold that the differences between man and woman are a fact of life. Better, therefore, is to recognize such personal convictions and traits for what they are, and to take them into consideration when conducting research. One way to work with any pre-set views we may have is to compensate for it by considering the views of fellow researchers. For instance, one might argue that a research project on underground rap music is best to be undertaken by students who share the age, background, and culture of those rappers. But such an **insider's perspective** could cause researchers to overlook certain aspects because they feel they are so self-evident that they are not worth considering or registering. Positionality can then be helpful, but more helpful might be to invite an **outsider's perspective**: why not call in a white middle-aged person who has little affinity with the subject but who may therefore ask the questions considered trivial by the insider? Such a diversity of views and experiences may provide a more profound understanding of the topic of study.

> The concept of **positionality** holds that students of Humanities need to reflect on their own position on the topic of research.

Positionality is not only important when researching people, but also when researching ideas, processes or texts. Imagine the Argentinian student reading Japanese literature, or the Norwegian scholar analysing South-African political speeches, or the non-believer studying religious texts. They may all run the risk of missing essential elements because they have no intimate knowledge of their topic of study. Still, their outsider's perspective may yield interesting insights. The main task for any scholar, therefore, is to have some self-awareness in their approach of such texts (positionality), and to refer to other views (diversity). Just as multidisciplinarity brings in the different views from various academic disciplines, diversity of researchers may bring different perspectives of the same issue or event.

It must be noted that the notions of the insider and outsider can be used in two ways. The *researcher* can be an insider or outsider to the people or ideas that are being researched. This is what positionality refers to. But the insider or outsider approach can also apply to the *method of research*: does the researcher merely describe people or ideas or does the researcher follow their inner logic and epistemology. The first is called the etic approach whereby the researcher takes the position of an observing outsider who contents with observing, recording and describing. The second is called the emic approach whereby the researcher tries to capture the inside perspectives of the people or ideas under study.

> In the **etic** approach the researcher takes the position of an observing outsider. In the **emic** approach the researcher tries to capture the inside perspectives of the people or ideas under study.

Diversity of views

While the student of International Studies may be aware of any bias or preconceived notions, they furthermore also need to consider any views they may encounter that are different from their own. This diversity of views may be confusing to some and interesting to others, but academically they can be used to the student's advantage when trying to understand global complexities, as the following examples may illustrate:

Geography

Our place of origin or residence determines our sense of location on the globe. That place is the center of our world and serves as the reference point when using words like 'far' and 'nearby', or 'north' or 'east'. While these terms may seem objectively descriptive, they can also be quite normative. For instance, to speak of the North and the South in the world is not only an indication of place. In the past decades, it has also referred to socioeconomic standing: the North stood for rich and developed and the South for poor and underdeveloped. Nowadays, this dichotomy has acquired

Figure I.5.1 World map

a political-historical meaning: the 'global North' stands for rich, former colonial countries that allegedly want to maintain their privileges, while the 'global South' stands for former colonies that are trying to get a place at the international table.

Generation

Generations look at the world differently: the older generations have seen things happen, the younger generations see things in the making. The stereotype would then be that the older generations are conservative ('we stick to what we know') while the younger generations are ambitious ('we need to make changes'). A famous proverb has it that 'If you're not a liberal when young, you have no heart. If you're not a conservative when old, you have no brain.' But there is more. Usually, global events which take place during one's late teens and early twenties determine one's world view: in my case, I belong to the Cold War generation, raised with fear of 'the bomb', while I see how the generations of students passing before me today are imprinted by terrorism in the 2010s, a pandemic in the 2020s, and have an overall angry desperation about climate change. These are historical imprints that determine the concerns and actions of each generation.

History

People may have radically different perceptions of the same history. What is a 'liberation' organization to one, may be a 'terrorist' organization to the other. Europeans consider the conquests of Alexander the Great and the Romans as the spread of civilization, while they perceive the conquests by Arabs and Ottomans as acts of aggression. From the perspective of the Chinese and the Mongols, the Aztecs and the Inca's, the British and the Spaniards, their conquests are seen as shows of power leading to grand civilizations, while others will perceive them as forces of destruction that obliterated entire cultures.

Social class

In my class of International Studies, I teach over 500 students whom together usually represent over fifty nationalities. An 'international classroom' indeed! But how diverse is such a class, really? They represent different cultures, and many of these students may be even bi- or multicultural, but the overall majority is middle or upper class. This is not a reproach – we are who we are – but these students need to face the fact that they represent a minority in the world and that their position in society may very well influence their view of the world.

Religion

It is tempting to judge a believer only on the merits of that person's belief thereby dissociating religion from its cultural environment (see also chapter 'Beliefs and belief systems'). But while religions may have their belief systems and epistemologies, every believer is also part of a local culture. Catholics in America, Brazil, Uganda and Korea may share the same faith but their different cultural backgrounds may affect their practices of that faith. We may view this as a form of glocalization of religions: their belief structures are global, but their local manifestations can be different, based on their cultural environment.

There are many more examples like these. Suffice it to conclude that the students of International Studies can only be successful in understanding the world 'out there' after proper self-reflection on their own cultural context 'in here'.

Further reading

Charles R. Hale, 'Introduction' in: Charles R. Hale (ed.), *Engaging Contradictions: Theory, Politics, and Methods of Activist Scholarship*, University of California Press, 2008

Fred Halliday, '"Orientalism" and Its Critics,' *British Journal of Middle Eastern Studies*, Vol. 20, No. 2, 1993, pp. 145-163

M. W Morris, D.A. Leung & B. Lickel, 'Views from inside and outside: Integrating Emic and Etic Insights about Culture and Justice Judgement', *Academy of Management Review*, 24(4), 1999, pp.781-796

Jeffrey Thomas Nealon and Susan Searls Giroux, Chapters 9 ('Posts') and 10 ('Differences'), *The Theory Toolbox: Critical Concepts for the Humanities, Arts, and Social Sciences*, Rowman & Littlefield Publishers, 2012

Edward Said, 'Introduction' (chapter), *Orientalism*, 1979

PART II
Global Structures

To understand the human dimensions of global complexities, the student of International Studies must understand the global structures that are in place in today's world. These are the mechanisms and organizational structures that are entrenched in our world and therefore shape the ways humankind operates. Some of these mechanisms and structures are as old as humankind, like migration, economy, patriarchy, arts, belief systems. Others are of a more recent date, like international agreements or intergovernmental organizations like the United Nations. A selection of seven global structures will be discussed in the following chapters.

CHAPTER 1

Beliefs and belief systems

A unique feature of humans is their ability to believe. They can believe to be member of a nation, they can believe in gods or stories of creation, in ideas and ideologies. Believing is the conviction that something is true. It is a driving force behind *ideas* as well as *identities*, which are two of the 3 I's. The act of believing has always been an elementary force that helps shape the way we see our world and the way people should interact. It can also be extremely powerful as a force that drives people to act. For instance, wars are often caused by ideas that people feel strongly about. One such idea may be that they are superior and therefore entitled to rule others, or that their nation is under threat, or that a 'motherland' needs to be reunited. Similarly, enormous monuments are erected, wholly or in part to celebrate a belief, like the pyramids of Egypt and Central America, the Roman and Greek temples, the gothic churches of Europe, the Buddhas of Bamyan in Afghanistan, Ankor Wat in Cambodia, the Boru Budur in Indonesia, to name but a few.

Monumental belief

In Göbekli Tepe in Turkey, remains have been found of monumental buildings of stone, with carved pillars of five meters and six to seven tons in weight. They date from 11.500 years ago (that is twice as old as Stonehenge in England that dates 5.500 years back, and almost three times older than the pyramids in Egypt that date 4.500 years back). It was the period that people started to settle in larger agricultural communities. Since these buildings do not seem to have any practical use, archaeologists think they may have had a religious purpose.

We call a belief a **belief system** when the beliefs and belief practices of a people are structured and organized. The notion of beliefs is usually equated with religions. Examples of religious belief systems are Judaism, Christianity and Islam, that have elaborate traditions of rituals and scriptural scholarship. Other religious belief systems are less structured (like Hinduism) or focus more on oral transmissions (like many 'indigenous' religions). Belief systems other than religious ones include ideologies like capitalism, communism or fascism. In some instances, even certain cultural customs and practices are considered belief systems. (See below for a discussion on the relation between religion and culture, and between religion and ideology.)

While a belief *system* can emerge, evolve and disappear, the underlying activity of *believing* is a distinct mechanism that is entrenched in humanity, and therefore a global structure.

> A **belief** is a conviction about something that one holds to be true. A **belief system** elaborates a belief in a coherent set of doctrines, concepts and rituals.

> **'Dreaming'**
> Aboriginal peoples in Australia have an oral tradition that is often referred to as 'Dreaming'. By means of song, knowledge is preserved and transmitted about a variety of topics, like mythology, law, kinship, and medicine. When this knowledge is about navigating land routes on the ground as well as paths in the sky, these are referred to as 'Dreaming Tracks' (also: 'Songlines').

Horizontal and vertical bonds

When someone believes in intangible powers beyond oneself (transcendental powers), this creates a bond between that person and a larger order which may be referred to as divine creation, a cosmic order or a universal truth. It is a bond that may lead to a belief system, like Judaism or Hinduism, or to a mythology, like the ones of the Greeks, the Babylonians or the Mayas, or to a universal order like human rights. We may imagine this as a vertical bond of believing, that is, between a person 'down here' and a higher order 'out there'.

We can also imagine a horizontal bond of believing, that is, among people. We believe in each other, we believe in the legends and myths of our ancestors, we believe in the values and traditions that we find typical for our community. This kind of belief is what shapes people's identities, whether it is religious, cultural, ethnic or something else. This kind of belief creates a bond among people and acts as the glue that keeps communities together.

It has become common practice to distinguish between the vertical and horizontal bonds as 'religion' and 'society', respectively, whereby society is usually marked as 'neutral' or 'secular', meaning non-religious. For that reason, they are often considered to be two separate realms. However, this view is typical for Western epistemology. In most societies, religion plays an intricate role in the daily lives of people, combining rather than separating the transcendental ('vertical') and the daily practical ('horizontal').

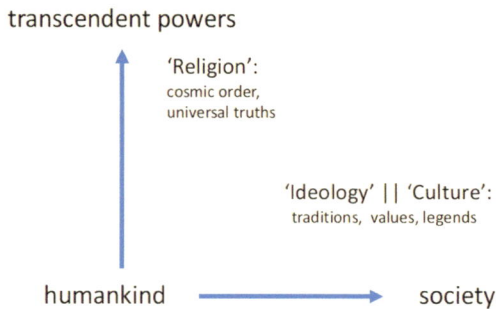

Figure II.1.1 Separating religion and society

Ideology or religion?

This distinction between vertical and horizontal bonds may help explain the difference between religion and ideology. The ways people believe in and practice their religious faith can sometimes be very similar to the ways people believe in and practice communism. What then is the difference between the two? Is communism not like religion, or is Christianity not like an ideology? The distinction between ideology and religion can be illustrated with the notion of 'vertical' and 'horizontal' beliefs. Religion is the ('vertical') belief of people in something 'out there' and deals with transcendent forces and spirituality, and wonders about the meaning of life. An ideology, on the other hand, deals with the practicalities of life on earth, the here and now, and as such is a belief in human ('horizontal') relations. This admittedly schematic differentiation can become blurred when religious views are being interpreted and expressed in norms and rules that regard society and politics. We see this happening today with Hinduism in India, Judaism in Israel, Islam in countries like Iran and Saudi-Arabia, Christianity in America. In those instances, it may be justified to term these uses of religion as ideology.

Culture or religion?

A similar discussion exists about the relation between religion and culture. However, this is a distinction that is often harder to make. An example to illustrate this is female genital mutilation (FGM), also euphemistically called 'female circumcision'. The severe forms of this practice are widespread in several African countries where it has been a custom for thousands of years, and it is still widely practiced by Muslims as well as Christians and people of other religions. It could therefore be argued this custom is not religion-specific. However, the practice is so deeply imbedded in the local culture of these people, that they consider it a religious imperative, even when religious leaders have publicly and clearly stated that this practice is *not* part of their respective religions. People apparently feel so strongly about it, that they believe they are held by a higher order or power to continue carrying it out.

FGM shows how culture and religion can be intertwined. Does it matter then whether we call something culture or religion? From the perspective of believing in something, both culture and religion can have the same importance to people. From that viewpoint, the terms religion and culture can be used interchangeably. On the other hand, there is a distinct difference between culture and religion regarding the *source* of that belief. Simply put, a culture is shaped by the norms and rituals to which one is accustomed ('this is how we do things here'), while religion, especially as a belief system, is shaped by what divine authorities are assumed to have ordained ('this is what my religion requires'). In practice, these two may very well overlap in the strength of their beliefs, but the motivation of the two is different.

Countries with the highest FGM-rates:	
Somalia	99%
Guinea	95%
Djibouti	90%
Mali	89%
Egypt	87%
Sudan	87%
Eritrea	83%
Sierra Leone	83%
Gambia	73%
Ethiopia	65%
Mauretania	64%
(UNICEF, *Female Genital Mutilation Database*, 2023)	

Beliefs and the state

Throughout human history, religion has played on important role for rulers of empires and states. And more recently, in the twentieth century we see how ideologies – especially socialism and communism – have played a similar role. Below, we will focus on religion as it has a longer legacy and, so it seems, still has a stronger impact than ideologies (many states halfway through the 20th century who called themselves socialist are now emphatically referring to a religious identity, including Russia, Poland and Egypt). In its relationship with the state, religion assumes four roles that are sometimes separate, but mostly overlapping:

First, religion is used **to legitimize state rule**. Kings and leaders have often felt the need for endorsement from higher powers to legitimize their rule. To achieve that, the ultimate leadership of rulers was framed in terms of a God-given rule (or, like in China, a mandate from heaven). Nowadays, in most states, this connection with higher powers has been legally severed, and the legitimacy of rulers officially rests no longer on something that is God-given, but on the will of the people. Still, quite a few rulers today feel the need to show that they are close to religion and its institutions.

Figure II.1.2 President Trump and religious community leaders

The second role that religion plays is as the identity of a people, empire or country. In most instances this is made official by naming a religion the **state religion**. This usually means that other religions are allowed, but that the state religion serves as the identity for that state. This has, in the past, also had consequences for the legal and social structure of such countries. The state religion would set the basic rules of that society. For instance, changing religions would be considered laudable when converting to the state religion, but possibly punishable when converting to another religion. Another aspect of religion that was very prominent in the past was that most societies were organized along religious lines: religious segregation was very common, with people belonging to the state religion taking up prominent positions, and people usually marrying within their own religious community and living in their own towns or city quarters in accordance with their own religious customs.

This all changed dramatically in the nineteenth century when, starting in Europe and then gradually spreading to most of the world, the notion of **citizenship** was introduced (a global trend which now has become a global structure). This was a radical break with a centuries-old tradition in which religion usually determined the social fabric of society: the introduction of citizenship meant that all citizens were considered equal, regardless of their religion. The consequences were enormous, because from then on every citizen, regardless of their religion, could obtain social positions that were previously reserved for those who belonged to the state religion. Most states today recognise that equality, although it is often more in rule than in practice: many countries will not have a president with a religion different from that of the majority population or from the state religion.

The third role of religion is that of **guardian of morality**. That which is good or wrong in a given society was usually phrased in religious terms. Nowadays, most states try to pass laws and regulations that are allegedly of a more 'neutral' or otherwise non-religious nature. But still, the overlap remains. For instance, those who oppose the legalization of abortion are mostly not arguing from the legal point of view that killing is a crime, but from the moral and religious point of view that life is sacred.

The fourth role is that of **religion as an institution**. These institutions arose to teach and guide people in their religion, to serve them in performing rituals, to provide them with counsel, to legitimize the rule of state leaders and to determine what is good and what is bad. In doing so, these institutions became powerful actors themselves, whether by their association with the most important state institutions or as actors in civil society. Throughout history and to this day, there have always been tensions between religious institutions and state governments because they both need each other, but also want to keep their independence. Both of them combined in one person is rare today, the most conspicuous examples being the pope (leader of both the Catholic Church and the Vatican) and the supreme leader of Iran.

Secularism and secularization

Two terms need explanation since they are often used interchangeably but have entirely different meanings. **Secularization** is the social process whereby religion becomes less important to the believers and so plays an increasingly lesser role in that society. Whereas secularization has to do with people's relationship with religion, secularism has to do with the state's relationship with religion. **Secularism** is a manner in which the state distances itself from religion.

Confusing about the terms secularization and secularism is that their adjectives are the same: 'secular'. When a state or a person is called secular, it can refer to secularization as well as secularism. A 'secular state' can mean that a state wants to keep government and religion separate, but it can also mean that the people of that state are not very religious. To complicate matters, 'secular' is often used to denote non-religious. That is not necessarily the case. Persons can be religious and secular at the same time: they can be very religious and do not want the state to interfere with their personal beliefs.

> **Secularization** relates to people: it is the process whereby religious thinking, practices and institutions lose their social significance. **Secularism** relates to the state: it is the legal and political way a state distances itself from religion. **'Secular'** is the adjective of both terms.

Another – mostly Western – alternative term for secularism is the expression **'separation of church and state'**. However, this expression is not clear as it manifests itself in three very distinct ways:

a) *The separation of government and religious institutions.* Religious institutions are not the same thing as belief systems or a community of believers: they are the organized forms of religious communities with a clergy, infrastructure, and offices. In a secular state, religious institutions and governments are assumed to operate independently from each other.

b) *The separation of religion and politics.* This relates to the degree that a country allows religion to be part of politics. In certain countries it is allowed to have religious political parties (like the many 'Christian Democratic' parties in Europe), in other countries that is strictly forbidden (like in France and, until recently, in Turkey).

c) *The separation of religion and the public domain.* This is when religion is reduced to a private affair that should preferably not be visible in the public domain. According to this principle, people are free to be religious, but they are not to show it in public. France is a typical example of this, as it actively bans expressions of religion from all public places that belong to the state, such as parliament, all public offices, post offices, state banks, public schools, and the like.

These three different manifestations of the 'separation of church and state' may help to navigate the complex ways in which each state has arranged its relationship with religion. Still, confusion about these relationships will remain. This is not only caused by the many different structures that exist in regulating this relationship, but also by the religious history and culture of each society. For example, The Netherlands and the United States both claim to uphold a system of secularism, but they are quite different in the manner they do this. The Netherlands has several explicitly religious political parties (Christian and Islamic), while the United States does not. However, in The Netherlands one finds very little if any religious discourse in the public or political domain, as opposed to the States. This is not a result of a political or legal order, but of custom: the Dutch have a culture where religion is not considered part of the public or political domain, while in the United States religion is customarily very much part of the public and political domain

Further reading

Peter L. Berger, *The Sacred Canopy: Elements of Sociological Theory of Religion*, Anchor, 1990.

Jose Casanova, *Global Religious and Secular Dynamics*, Brill, 2019

Clifford Geertz, "Chapter 4: Religion as a cultural system" in *The Interpretation of Cultures: selected essays*, Fontana Books, 1993

Jeffrey Haynes (ed.), *Handbook on Religion and International Relations*, Edward Elgar Publishing, 2021

Mark Juergensmeyer "The Worldwide Rise of Religious Nationalism", *Journal of International Affairs*, Vol. 50, No. 1 (Summer 1996), pp. 1-20

Rhys H. Williams "Religion as Political Resource: Culture or Ideology?" *Journal for the Scientific Study of Religion*, Vol. 35, No. 4 (December 1996), pp. 368-378

CHAPTER 2

Economics

Interests, or the first 'I' of the 3-Is, encompasses a wide variety of domains, ranging from what sustains a person (food, energy, clothes, shelter) to what makes life livable (medical care, body care, education) and enjoyable (sports, arts, leisure). Providing for these interests is done by managing the production and distribution of resources and goods. The management of the production, distribution and consumption of such goods is called economy. These activities have always been part of the lives of humankind. People have structured their economic activities on individual, communal, national and global levels.

> **Economy** refers to the way in which people provide for their needs. **Economics** is the name of the academic discipline that studies how and why people make decisions about production and distribution of goods and services.

Economic systems

An economy is a mechanism that balances the needs of people with their resources (land, ores, oil, water – see chapter 'Resources and Climate'), their 'inventories' (raw materials, foodstuffs, product parts) and 'capital' (everything needed for production, like human labor and ingenuity, tools, machines, factories, transport). Important in this equation are the people themselves: they determine their needs and what must be produced to cater to those needs, just as their qualities and abilities will determine if and how they manage to produce what needs to be produced. These needs can be stimulated by technology (think of inventions like agriculture, machines, mobile phones), but also by *ideas* (such as the prohibition or the encouragement of certain foods or practices like veganism, religious dietary laws, religious bans on electricity or vaccination).

The ideal situation would be the perfect balance of needs and resources so that people can live a good life. To reach that balance, people developed various types of economies. The early forms were **pastoral**, **trade-based** and **agriculture-based** economies to be joined later by the **industry-based** economy. How these economies were implemented and how they evolved, differed depending on time and place. While pastoral economies gradually disappeared with time, the other three economic systems became increasingly global and very few countries today have a national economy that is fully self-sustainable ('autarkic').

With the emergence of states and industrialized forms of production, two other types of economy developed. One is the **planned economy** in which governments regulate production and therefore consumption. In this system, people only participate in the production process in positions that are allocated to them, and their consumption is usually rationed. The other type is known as the **market economy**, in which the government plays a minimal role, and the production and consumption of goods are left to the needs and initiatives of the people. Of course, these are two archetypes of economic systems, and most of today's economies are a mixture of the two. But these are not economic systems of their own accord: they are put in place by people or, more commonly, their governments. The manner in which economies are shaped stem from *ideas* that people have on how best to manage them.

Ideas about economy

Economists and ideologues have come up with various ideas on how an economy could be organized to best serve the interests of society. In the nineteenth century, two models emerged that still apply today, albeit with many adaptations. Key to these models are the notion of private ownership and the role of the state.

The first model is **capitalism**. It is based on the notion of private ownership, meaning that the capital (labor, tools, money, etc.) needed for production is privately owned and its owners are free to decide what to do with that capital. The state ideally plays no role in the regulation of the market or in labor rights, nor in environmental, ethical or public health issues. That's why capitalism is usually found in market-based economies. In such economies, however, different choices can be made regarding the financial involvement of the state in matters of education, housing, healthcare and infrastructure. While these choices are matters of political debate, all states nowadays agree that the organization and costs for the protection of the country (judiciary, army and police) are the exclusive domain of the state.

The second model is **communism**. Communism was a response to some of the excesses of the capitalist system whereby people without capital (who represented the largest part of the population) depended on those with capital. This disparity led to poverty among the greater working population and excessive wealth among the few who owned the capital. That is why the communist model denounced private ownership and stipulated that all capital should be jointly owned by those who did the work (the working class). The entire population of a country should become a single working class, and the state, as the representative of the population, must administer and manage the joint ownership of capital. While in name the people own all the capital, the state has a central role in regulating anything that has to do with the economy. One of the downsides of such a system of planned economy was that various communist states made political or economic miscalculations in regulating the production of goods. For instance, the Soviet Union emphasized the development of heavy industry in the 1930s which resulted in famine because there were not enough resources left for agriculture.

Nowadays, most states use hybrid forms of these two systems, whereby the main question is always how much (or how little) power the state should hold in regulating the economy. Choices made in this respect are always driven by *interests* and *ideas* and are therefore highly political. For that reason, matters of the economy are often connected to ideas about **freedom**. Countries that embrace 'political' freedoms and consequently refrain from interfering in people's opinions or organizations, also tend to hold back in matters of the economy. On the other hand, a country that embraces 'social' freedoms, might regulate matters of the economy with the purpose of a 'fair' distribution of wealth which may leave people little freedom to determine that for themselves. Governments often try to find the middle ground.

The road to serfdom or freedom?

Economist Friedrich Hayek is one of the godfathers of neoliberalism, advocating free market in *The Road to Serfdom* (1944), with the argument that state control of economic decision-making would lead to oppression of freedoms. Economist and Nobel prize winner Joseph Stiglitz argues in *The Road to freedom* (2024) that neoliberalism has led to the freedom of a few to oppress the many, and that the state needs to play an active role to guarantee civil liberties.

Market and trade

Rare is the situation that a person or household or community is completely self-sustainable. The same applies today to states: few, if any, have all the wealth, including the human resources, to meet the needs of its population. Usually, there is an imbalance between what is produced and what is needed. Exchange, or **trade**, is a way to compensate for this imbalance: what one needs is imported from elsewhere, and what one has in surplus can be exported. Trade has always been a part of humankind, and the many ancient trade routes across continents and seas show that consumptive needs were such that it paid off to get the wanted goods from afar.

The imbalance between that which is produced and that which is needed could be compensated for by **diversification**, that is to generate as many different types of products as possible to reduce the dependence on importing what is lacking. However, some economic theories argue that diversification weakens one's economic position, and therefore advocate the opposite, **specialization**: a country should focus on its primary resources or production capabilities and use it for export, the proceeds of which can then be used to buy and import all the goods the country needs. For that reason, countries like Egypt and Uzbekistan converted much of their agriculture to cotton in the 1950s, Vietnam to coffee in the 1980s, and so on. Specialisation also contributed to an increase in global trade: for instance, Taiwan is one of the few producers of semiconductor chips and is the main exporter of these chips across the world just like Brazil is the world's number one exporter of soybeans (60% of the world trade).

> **Rentier state** is the name for a state whose income relies almost exclusively on the export of a single product for which little labor is required, like oil or gas. Such a state is said to live of the rent revenues of that product. When the income is such that no national production is needed (because the 'rent' income is so high that everything can be bought), then the 'rentier' situation is considered disruptive for the domestic economic situation, and often also for the social-political situation.

The result of an imbalance between what people have and what they need creates a **market** that is driven by supply and demand. The changes in supply and demand influence the price of the commodity at hand. If the demand for a product increases, but supply cannot keep up with demand, the price that consumers are willing to pay will rise. This mechanism can even itself out in time, but in complex societies states will often feel the need to interfere with the market: governments may stockpile certain products or set prices, raise tariffs against foreign goods or provide subsidies.

Impact of a global economy

The increasing interconnectedness of economies today has had an impact on the world in unprecedented ways, both positively and negatively.

The main example of the negative impact is that interconnectedness can also lead to interdependence. This showed in the financial crisis of 2008, which was sparked by defaults on subprime mortgage loans in the United States which triggered a near meltdown of banking systems across the world. Another example is the climate. The more companies rely on importing and exporting across the world, the more the transports needed for that will have an impact on the climate. The so-called carbon (or environmental, or energy) footprint has become the indicator of such an impact. With increasing concern about climate change, pressure has mounted on consumers as well as producers to be careful of that footprint.

Belt and Road Initiative

For centuries the 'Silk Route' existed across Asia, consisting of myriad routes linking up to a commercial highway connecting Eastern Europe with Central and Eastern Asia. In 2013, China coined the term 'Silk Road Economic Belt' (later: 'Belt and Road Initiative') for an extensive program of investments and development with numerous countries in Asia, Africa and Europe, creating a network of transport and cooperation.

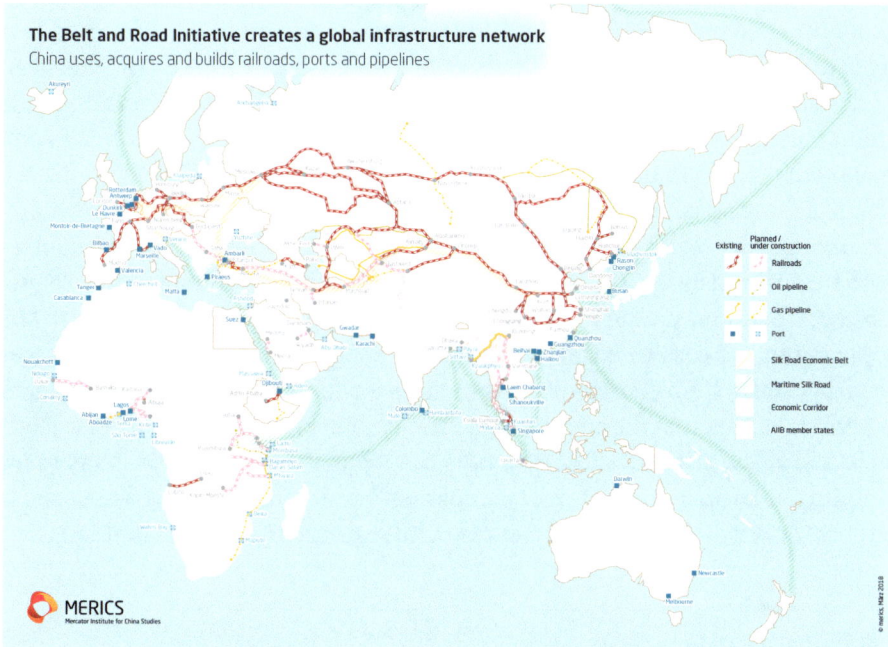

Figure II.2.1 China Belt and Road Initiative

The global economy also has its advantages. The main advantage is for companies: they have easy access to resources, parts and production, and they have more flexibility in allocating production. For instance, they can move their entire enterprise to another country because the local salaries or legal environment there are considered more beneficial. While this will create job opportunities in the new countries where production facilities are started, it also creates unemployment in the country that is being left. Another advantage of the global economy is the wide availability of products. This has contributed, for instance, to an increase in food production that, together with agricultural innovations, allowed for sustaining a rapidly rising world population.

The global economy has also raised the concern that certain products and brands may lose their typical 'national' identity once they are being reproduced across the world (like French wine and Greek feta cheese), or when they are assembled outside of their country of origin (like Swedish Volvo and Japanese Nintendo). For some of these products, the national brand is considered of the essence, causing the rise of lobbies to protect the national naming of these products.

It may look like individual consumers are crushed in these global developments, but the contrary is true. Consumers have united in international pressure groups that boycott certain products to force companies to change their methods. This is happening in the case of coffee, for instance, where consumers are encouraged to only drink coffee from companies that treat the coffee workers fairly. Similar actions are undertaken against the sweat shops in South-East Asia that produce the clothing that is sold at low prices in Western stores. Such pressure is also increasingly exerted for political reasons: international companies like McDonalds and Starbucks have been boycotted for their commercial ties with countries like China and Israel.

Economy and democracy
During the 1990s, there was a general assumption among mostly Western countries that democracy was the prerequisite for a functioning economy. Southeast Asian countries, however, showed that a flourishing economy could be achieved without fulfilling the conditions of democracy.

Criticism

Economic thinking has received its share of criticism from economists and outsiders. Two types of criticism will be discussed here.

The first criticism regards the assumption that people act as the *homo economicus*, which refers to economic decision-making based on reasoned calculations. This assumption has allowed economists to construct models based on what were considered logical decision processes. The so-called behaviorists, however, have indicated the erratic and sometimes even irrational processes of human thinking, including in economic practices: their decisions are often based on instinct, bias, and emotions. The behaviorists have shown that rational decisions are usually the result of slow thinking processes while the emotional and instinctive decisions are made quickly. As a result, people do not necessarily act consistently and rationally in their economic actions: they may spend an extra hour in the car to drive to a store on the other side of town for a relatively small price advantage, or take high insurance for relatively cheap appliances, or are more willing to spend one hundred euros on several products that are on sale than the same one hundred euros on a single quality product that they really need. These 'cognitive illusions' appear to be the prime drivers of economic behavior rather than calculated rational consideration.

Brain 'kinks'

Professor Kahneman (died 2024) introduced the notion of universal brain "kinks" to indicate inconsistencies in economic thinking. Famous is the kink of 'loss-aversion' which means that loss hurts more than gain – for instance, the loss of $100 seems to hurt about twice as much as the gaining of $100 brings pleasure.

(Daniel Kahneman, *Thinking, Fast and Slow*, 2011)

Another criticism of economics as practiced today is that it deviates from its original goal, that is: organizing behavior to make people more comfortable and improve their well-being. Rather than being a means to an end, critics argue that economics has shifted to being the end itself. Their concern is that there is an increasing tendency to use the notion of 'economic growth' as a goal and justification in its own right, instead of using economics in such a way that it satisfies the needs that sustain the individual, community, or society. To put it in simple terms: greed has become the ingredient for what has become an immoral economy. One of the results of such economic systems is the increasing divide between the rich and the poor. Several economists, like Piketty and the Nobel prize winners Joseph Stiglitz, and Daron Acemoglu and Simon Johnson (who shared the 2024 Nobel prize), have pointed out how this inequality can become a source of disruption in today's democratic societies.

"When plunder becomes a way of life for a group of men living together in society, they create for themselves in the course of time a legal system that authorizes it and a moral code that glorifies it."

(Frederic Bastiat, economist, 1801-1850)

These two issues – the paradoxes of human (economic) behavior, and the misuse of economic systems – have been food for political debates about the question of how to distribute wealth fairly. But this question has also become a global challenge: how can one balance the coexistence on the same planet of extreme richness and poverty, and of food waste and famine? This will be partly discussed in the chapter 'Sustainable Development.'

Further reading

Daron Acemoglu and Simon Johnson, *Power and Progress: Our Thousand-Year Struggle Over Technology and Prosperity*, PublicAffairs, 2023

David N. Balaam, Bradford Dillman, *Introduction to International Political Economy*, Routledge, 2019

Abhijit V. Banerjee and Esther Duflo, *Poor Economics: The Surprising Truth about Life on Less Than $1 a Day*, Penguin, 2012

Thomas Piketty, *Capital in the 21st Century* (transl.), Brilliance, 2014

Kenneth A. Reinert, *An Introduction to International Economics. New Perspectives on the World Economy*, Cambridge University Press, 2020

Joseph Stiglitz, *The Road to freedom*, Norton & Co, 2024

CHAPTER 3

Nation and state

People tend to identify with their own kind, based on a shared ethnicity, culture, history, language, and religion. Here, the two I's of *ideas* and *identity* are the main bonding forces. What is unique about humans is that they also bond in this way in groups that are much larger than families or tribes and therefore surpass the number of people that can claim to know each other. When such large groups of people who are unknown to each other but nevertheless live together in a cohesive and enduring connection, they are often referred to as a **nation**.

A nation usually occupies a territory and can, but does not have to, be organized in a political unit. For instance, most **empires** encompassed several nations under the leadership of a single nation. Empires usually allowed religious and cultural differences to co-exist within its realm. The paradox of almost each empire was that they were established by violence and destruction but then continued by establishing their own civilization (often by using elements of the civilizations and cultures of the nations that were conquered). Empires have existed everywhere in the world, the first known empires dating from the 4th millennium BCE and the last ones being the European colonial empires (although it has been argued that hegemonical states like the United States and the Soviet Union also constituted empires, and the same is being said about certain corporate firms that are globally active).

Another type of political organization is the **nation-state** which assumes that its people form a single nation that shares a territory and shapes their nationhood by means of state education and national commemorations and religious holidays. Since the nineteenth century such nation-states have replaced empires, and emerged as the new world entity that expresses its desire for self-determination in a political unit called a state.

State and Empire

An **empire** is established by military force and encompasses large territories and many peoples. An empire can subsume one or more civilizations, and usually develops a new civilization within its realm.

A **state** can have two meanings: a) specific: a political unit that claims to have a single culture and people ('nation'); b) general: a political unit with an organized and complex form of governance (which may also apply to an empire, for instance).

Global structure and 3-I's

The nation-state has become so entrenched in today's world that it has become a global structure. This shows in several ways. First, all countries today express themselves as nation-states. The collapse of the last colonial empires resulted in the formation of numerous new states, so that the number of states has almost quadrupled since 1945.

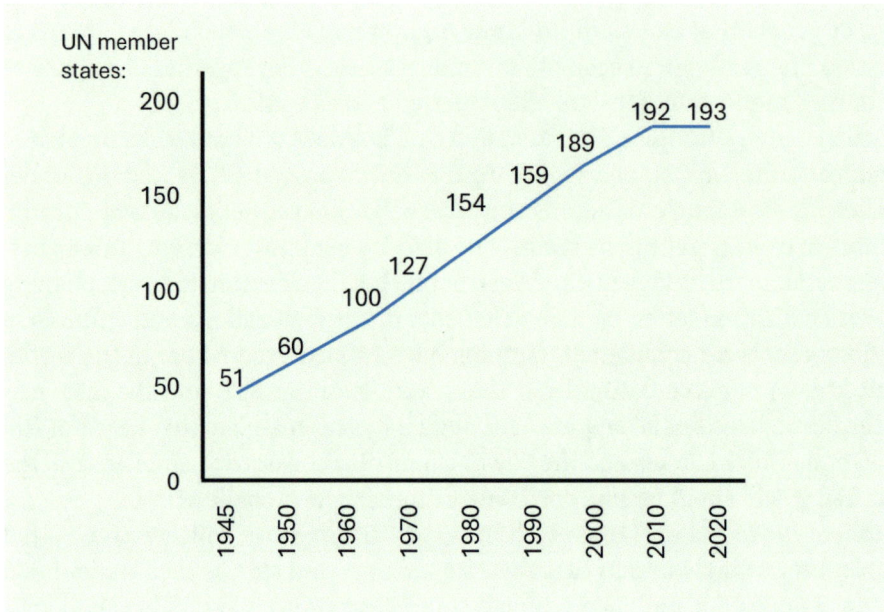

Figure II.3.1 The increase in number of states in the world

While many of these states may be based on civilizations and political units that had existed for centuries before they declared themselves states in the nineteenth and twentieth centuries, the novelty of the 'state' is its structure. All states in the world work with the same organizational blueprint of parliament-government-judiciary, and almost all states refer to themselves as 'of', 'for' or 'by' the people (many states named themselves 'republic'). Finally, states have become the main drivers of almost all international and global activity, as we will see in the following chapters. In doing so, an international playfield has been created in which states are the main players. Even states that oppose the domination of an international order or morality – like Iran, Russia, China – play by the rules of that playfield.

The famous sentence "**Government of the people, by the people, for the people**" by President Lincoln in 1863 refers to a government owned by the people ('of'), executed by the people ('by') and serving the people ('for').

All 3-I's – *interests, ideas, identities* – are powerful drivers behind the notion of a state. They explain the existence of a state: to pursue the interests of its people, to be organized and governed in accordance with certain ideas, and to bind the people in a national identity. The 3-I's are also helpful in explaining the actions of states towards each other. Such international relations are usually described in terms of interests: states trade, negotiate or wage war with each other in the pursuit of land, resources, and power. But ideas and identities are often just as important motivators for such interaction: national pride, political ideologies, religious or economic beliefs may push states to cooperate or to fight each other, just like identities – cultural, religious, linguistic, historical – can bring states together or push them apart.

States as we know them today have three important qualities. First, they have a connection with their population, which is often referred to as the 'nation'. Second, states have developed a strong sense of being an independent, self-regulating unit that retains power over all people and issues within its borders – a notion known as sovereignty. And third, almost all states of today are modelled on a similar organizational structure. These three qualities will be discussed in more detail below.

The nation

The term 'nation' has acquired two meanings: a people sharing a cultural bond, and a people sharing a socio-political union (like a state or a form of self-governance). Today's notion of the state assumes that these two – state and nation – conflate, but that is not always the case. Most states today will propagate their unity as a political nation, but very few consist of a single cultural nation. Also, all nations live in one state or another, but not all nations have their own state. The Kurds, for instance, are a nation with a strong sense of a shared history and culture and language, but they live in the states of Turkey, Syria, Iran, and Iraq, where they partake in the social-political unity of each of those states.

A **nation** is a people who share a culture, history, language, ethnicity, religion, and who identify as a member of that nation. Ideally, a nation has its own territory and political organization (**nation-state**). However, most states today are made up of various nations, and a nation often lives in various states.

By the late nineteenth century, the notion of **self-determination** emerged, that is the right of a nation to determine its own fate (see chapter 'Equality and Self-determination'). This concept has been realized in various forms of autonomy for nations ranging from limited self-rule to full independent governance. The term nation-state is used when a nation regulates its affairs within an independent socio-political structure with its own territory and institutions. Ideally, this nation should share both a cultural and political-social bond, but reality proves differently.

Nationality and nationalism

The political and cultural bonds that one may feel as a person belonging to a nation converge in the notion of **nationality**. Nationality comprises both a legal and a cultural identity. Being 'Japanese' or 'Argentinian' means that one is the holder of a passport of that country which grants certain rights and duties, but it can also mean that one feels a cultural bond with that country. The difference between the two may show in the situation of migrants obtaining the nationality of the country they migrated to. This raises questions of a cultural nature: a Nigerian who obtains Japanese nationality, is she Japanese? She may consider herself Japanese, and may even speak fluent Japanese and be well-acquainted with Japanese history and culture, but will her fellow Japanese accept her as such? Being a 'native' of a country sometimes seems to be an extra prerequisite for belonging to a nation, together with one's appearance. (See also chapters 'Migration', 'Identity', and 'Transnationalism'.)

'National minorities', 'ethnic minorities', and 'Indigenous Peoples'
A state that perceives itself as a single political and cultural nation will refer to 'other' nations within the state as 'national minorities': they share the (legal) nationality of everyone in the state, but not the cultural identity of the majority. Three types of such minorities can be discerned.

A **national minority** is the minority that belongs to a nation that has a state elsewhere. Examples are the Chinese in Indonesia, the Germans in Hungary, the Tajiks in Afghanistan. The presence of these national minorities can be caused by their migration, or by state formation whereby borders were re-drawn so that a nation was carved up among several neighbouring states.

An **ethnic minority** is a nation that lives in more than one state, like the Yoruba in Nigeria, Benin and Togo, or the Kurds in Turkey, Syria, Iran, and Iraq

Indigenous people are the people who are native to a land where other people have settled and taken over.

An important factor in the emergence of states as we know them today is **nationalism**. Nationalism is the oil in the process generating the bond that a nation feels to a state and vice versa. Key roles are played by *identity* and *ideas*. The nations and their states are of such size that what binds its people cannot be established by personal relationships and interests, as would be the case in smaller communities, but must be accomplished by ideas and identities that are shared by all. A nation can consist of millions of people, but they nevertheless share this feeling of belonging together and to the country in which they live. For this reason, nations and states are also called 'imagined communities'.

'Imagined communities'

Nationalism imagines nations to exist, it creates something new, something that has not necessarily existed before.

(Benedict Anderson, *Imagined Communities*, 1983)

Nationalism creates a bond among people who do not necessarily know each other. Unlike other 'isms', nationalism has no ideologues or worked-out ideologies. It emerged in Europe during the nineteenth century and became a *global trend* leading to the emergence of the state as we know it today. One effect of nationalism is that it is *exclusive*: it only applies to 'our own kind' and does not extend to others who have different cultures, languages, or religions, and it does not *want* to extend to those others. Here we see an important difference with the old empires that often contained many nations (although often the members of only one nation ruled). Nationalism has caused various instances of cultural domination of one nation over others (by imposing a single language and culture, for instance), sometimes even leading to **ethnic or religious cleansing** by removing other nations from the territory of the nation-state.

'Successful' ethnic cleansing

After several years of war, Greece and Turkey decided in 1923 that it was for the best to 'exchange' the peoples in each other's countries. And so, an estimated 1 million Turkish people in Greece (many who had lived there for centuries) were moved to Turkey, and an estimated 1,5 million Greeks in Turkey (many of whom traced their roots to the ancient Greek colonies of more than two millennia ago) were moved to Greece. In the light of violent ethnic and religious cleansing in the Balkans at that time, this was considered a successful diplomatic solution.

Nationalism emphasizes as well as reinforces the nation's bond by means of **national rituals and symbols**. Some of these are cultural traditions, others are religious celebrations, and some are new traditions that have been invented for that purpose. Some rituals and symbols also specifically focus on the state itself, like raising the flag, singing the national anthem, cheering the national sports team, or performing commemorative services at a monument of the Unknown Soldier who died for the country. In doing so, people emphasize their national bond (which may be considered problematic when some citizens of a state have affiliations with another nation – see chapter 'Transnationalism'). These expressions of celebrating statehood are today shared by all states.

> **'Invented traditions'**
> Many national traditions that countries today celebrate may "appear or claim to be old [but] are often quite recent in origin and sometimes invented."
> (Eric Hobsbawm, *The Invention of Tradition*, 1983)

Sovereignty

The second characteristic of today's state is **sovereignty**, that is the right and the power to have full say on everything that happens within the state's borders. Sovereignty is also explained as the principle that states should not interfere in each other's internal affairs. One of the questions that has arisen since the 1990s is whether a humanitarian catastrophe in a state may justify the intervention by other states without permission by the state where the catastrophe is taking place. Some argue that in such a cases humanitarian needs overrule sovereignty. This is a hotly contested issue that will be discussed in the chapter 'Security'.

Sovereignty also became a loaded issue with the emergence of international cooperation among states: when sovereign states agree to work together, does this mean they have to give up part of their sovereignty? We will see in chapter 'International organizations' that states are generally unwilling to do so. A similar discussion arose regarding *judicial* sovereignty, and the question of whether an international court can decide over issues pertaining to a state (see chapter 'International agreements'). Relinquishing parts of judicial sovereignty became more common in the second half of the twentieth century but it remains contested: for the United Kingdom it was one of the reasons to leave the European Union in 2020 because it did not want the European Court of Justice to decide on British matters, and for the United States of America it has been the reason not to sign numerous international treaties.

> **Sovereignty** is the right of states to manage their own national affairs in any way they see fit, without interference from other states.

Recognition

To be (or: to become) a sovereign state requires inward as well as outward action. Inwardly, people must organize themselves as a socio-political polity. To maintain the autonomy and independence of this polity, outward action is required in terms of international relations, often bolstered with the armed capacity to defend that independence if need be. In the 20th century, a new element was added to being a state: recognition by other states. This can create complex and paradoxical situations: what if a state has established sovereignty but is not recognized as such (Somaliland)? What if a nation is recognized as a state even though it is not a functioning state (Palestine)? What if most states want to recognize a state but decide not to do so as not to antagonize one of the great powers (Taiwan)?

Recognition as a state

There are functioning states that are member the United Nations even though they are not recognized by all world states, like Israel (not recognized by 30 of the 193 world states) or Kosovo (not recognized by 49 of the 193 world states). Taiwan is a fully functioning state but is not a member of the United Nations and is only recognized by 12 states (a situation that created under pressure by China). Palestine is an example of a state that is not functioning as a full state, and that is not member of the United Nations, but that by 2025 was recognized by 145 of the 193 world states.

International recognition and (military) state power make up for an uneasy balance. History is rife with examples of states that conquered (parts of) other states whereby these conquered lands, in due time, became accepted as part of the conquering state. Nonetheless, a state may incorporate parts of other states by means of military power and claim that this land is now part of their state, even though it is not recognized by the majority of world states (examples are Russia in Ukraine and Georgia, Israel in Gaza, Golan, East Jerusalem and the Westbank). Opposed to one state claiming a territory, the reverse can also happen, that is, when a territory (and its people) claim independence from the state to which it officially belongs. The world states recognized this claim to independence by Timor-Leste from Indonesia (2002), for instance, but not by Catalonia from Spain (2019).

Figure II.3.2 In 1976, Burnum Burnum of the Wurundjeri tribe planted the Aboriginal flag in the shores of Dover and symbolically claimed England: "In claiming this colonial outpost, we wish no harm to you natives."

Micro-states and Micro-nations

Micro-states is the term for states that are very small in size and population (examples are Andorra, Comoros, Tuvalu). **Micro-nation** is the term commonly used for tiny entities, sometimes not more than rocks in the sea or a piece of land the size of several football fields, that claim independence. They often make a point of having their own flag, national anthem, and stamps. No one takes them seriously, and they are usually dismissed as a laughing matter. But they do touch upon the fundamental question what it means to become a sovereign state. Examples are North Dumpling Island (Conn., US); Conch Republic (Florida, US); Freetown Christiana (Denmark); Republic of Saugeais (France); Principality of Seborga (Italy), Principality of Hutt River (Australia).)

Organization of a state

Almost all states today have a similar organizational structure. What follows is a brief outline of the main elements of this organizational structure. The emphasis hereby will be on the Humanities perspective, both externally and internally.

Externally, we see that states often behave like human organisms, with emotions of pride, rage, fear, and so on. This is the stuff of (national) identity, which is a powerful mover of states. Internally, we see a similar dynamic whereby the various state organs can operate as actors by themselves.

Trias politica

Almost all states today adhere to the organizational structure of *trias politica*, the nineteenth century concept of a division between the executive (government), the legislative (parliament) and the judicial (courts) power. This was considered the best form of government and apparently is still considered to be so as all states are structured along these lines. If it is all functioning well, then an important condition is fulfilled of what today we call 'good governance' (see chapter 'Democracy and good governance'). But reality can be very different. This is because of what people do with these structures. There can be wide discrepancies between the structures as outlined on paper and the manners in which they function in practice. But today even the most autocratic rulers feel the need to legitimize their rule by paying lip service to the *trias politica*.

Bureaucracy

The civil service, better known as the bureaucracy, is a governmental power that is often underestimated. Civil servants are not elected, and they represent continuity while governments come and go. That is why they are also called the 'fourth power', in addition to the three official powers of government, parliament, and judiciary.

Civil society

States are usually divided between the state institutions and the people. In quite a few states the people are given a rather passive role, as the power is exercised by the institutions, and people can only let their voice be heard during elections. However, people often organize themselves (unless the state represses this) in parties, unions, organizations, churches, communities, clubs, and so on. The aims of these organizations can be very different: it can be to influence politics, do business, help the poor, play sports, promote culture, discuss current events. But the main feature of all these organized activities is that they are undertaken not by the government but by the people themselves. All this activity together is called **civil society** which is also described as a **public sphere** that hovers between the population and their governing institutions.

According to **Civil Society Theory**, the notion of civil society can explain the mechanisms of democracy. This theory argues that civil society is beneficial to a thriving democracy because the more people organize themselves, the more they discuss, criticize, promote and support certain issues that they find important, the more a country will become governed by and for the people. In the 1990s this theory became popular among policy makers in Western countries who promoted the support for civil society in non-democratic countries to enhance the formation of democratic structures in those countries (see chapter 'Democracy').

> "**Civil society** is composed of those more or less spontaneously emergent associations, organizations and movements that, attuned to how societal problems resonate in the private life spheres, distill and transmit such reactions in amplified form to the public sphere. The core of civil society comprises a network of associations that institutionalizes problem-solving discourses on questions of general interest inside the framework of organized public spheres."
>
> (Jürgen Habermas, *Between Facts and Norms*, 2004 (repr. from 1996), p. 367)

Social movements

The concept of civil society may explain the workings of democracy, but it does not explain why people rally for a cause, take to the street to demonstrate, or find other ways to pressure governments to make social or political changes. To study these phenomena, the Humanities uses the notion of social movements. A social movement is not an organization as we might find in civil society; a social movement emerges – often spontaneously and unexpectedly – and is loosely organized. While civil societies usually function on a national level only, social movements may take on global proportions. Examples are the climate movement, the anti-globalization movement, Black Lives Matter, #MeToo. Social movements are mostly mass movements, and, of course, members and organizations of civil society participate in them. For instance, the choirs and music organizations of Estonian civil society participated in the independence movement of 1990, just as the student unions participated in the Hong Kong demonstrations of 2019, and in the climate movement we find many established civil society organizations that work on sustainable development, nature preservation and ecology.

Social Movement Theories

'Social Movement Theories' (or 'SMT') stands for various theories that try to explain the mechanisms of social movements. The wide variety of SMT theories is a result of the variety of questions that are addressed: What is the goal of these movements? What is the opportunity that made the movement happen? What is the diagnosis of the issue that movement is protesting for (or against), and does it present solutions? Do the members of the movement share an identity?

Further reading

Benedict Anderson, *Imagined Communities. Reflections on the Origins and spread of Nationalism* (1983), Verso Books, 2016

Craig Calhoun, 'Civil Society/Public Sphere: History of the Concept' in *International Encyclopedia of the Social & Behavioral Sciences*: *Second Edition*, Elsevier, 2015, pp.701-706

Eric Hobsbawm and Terence Ranger (eds.), *The Invention of Tradition* (1983), Cambridge University Press, 2002

Jim Mac Laughlin, *Reimagining the Nation-State. The Contested Terrains of Nation-Building*, Pluto Press, 2001

Walter C. Opello and Stephen J. Rosow, *The Nation-State and Global Order: A Historical Introduction to Contemporary Politics*, Lynne Riener, 2004

Philip G. Roeder, *Where Nation-States Come From: Institutional Change in the Age of Nationalism*, Princeton University Press, 2007

Philipp Ther, *The Dark Side of Nation-States. Ethnic Cleansing in Modern Europe*, Berghahn, 2014

CHAPTER 4

Non-state actors

The term 'non-state actors' denotes organizations or even individual people that operate independently of states and that possess considerable power that may sometimes even compete with that of states. It is a relatively new term for an ancient phenomenon. Think of banking families, the elite societies of aristocracy, international trading companies, the networks of monasteries, and organized crime organizations. These kinds of organizations have been operating for centuries all around the world. Since the second half of the 20th century, however, the number and diversity of non-state actors that are active globally has grown exponentially.

> **International non-state actors** are organizations or individuals that a) are largely or entirely autonomous from central government control, b) originate from civil society, market economy, or from political impulses beyond state control, and c) operate as, or participate in networks which extend across the boundaries of at least two or more states.

There are different types of international non-state actors. Well-known are the organizations set up by people from various civil societies, like Amnesty International, Green Peace, or the Red Cross. Such non-state actors are commonly called 'non-governmental organizations' (NGOs) and often combine working locally, nationally, and globally at the same time. NGOs based on motivations of faith – often referred to as 'faith-based organizations' (FBOs) – form a special type of NGO. Other examples of non-state actors that operate on a global scale are commercial corporations and criminal and terrorist organizations. Some even argue that certain individual billionaires who are acting internationally, whether as entrepreneurs or as benefactors, can be considered non-state actors. The same may be said of individuals with great charisma, like the Pope and the Dalai Lama, or people like Ghandi or Mandela. One might describe these people and organizations as civil society on a global scale.

> **Non-governmental organizations** (or NGOs) are organizations set up by civil society and operate independently from the state. NGOs that are motivated by faith are also called **faith-based organizations** (or FBOs). Some NGOs work only locally or nationally, others also globally.

Impact

The impact that today's international non-state actors have on the world depends on the type of their activities:

Humanitarian causes

Organizations that focus on humanitarian causes, like human rights, development, ecological wellbeing, anti-racism, and the like, have their greatest impact by **raising awareness** in the general public and state governments. In some instances, this has been successful: human rights have become part of international politics and national laws, the United Nations has set development goals, and climate change has become part of the international political agenda, to name a few examples. That is quite an achievement. The non-state actors have been able to make many states and large segments of the general public aware of these situations and, sometimes, prompted them to undertake action.

Some NGOs focus on **conflict resolution**. The impact of these activities seems to be limited, however, as it is usually the states that play leading roles in finalizing the resolution of a conflict. Still, in the processes leading up to these conflict resolutions, it is often individuals who have the greatest impact, although their work is mostly unseen by the outside world. The abolition of apartheid in South Africa in 1991, for instance, or the Oslo accords of 1993 between Palestine and Israel, or the Good Friday agreement in 1998 between the United Kingdom and the IRA, were the result of years of quiet, patient work by individuals, often aided by outsiders that acted as mediators and go-betweens. The states were the ultimate peacemakers in these conflicts, but they could not have done so without the help of these (mostly individual) non-state actors.

Impact of Faith-Based Organizations

A 2022 study shows that the 'faith-aligned impact' of FBOs in terms of world finance is quite significant: approximately US$ 5 trillion. The breakdown is as follows: Islamic capital ($ 4 trillion), Dharmic capital ($ 300 billion), Christian capital ($ 260 billion), Jewish capital ($ 160 billion). However, these numbers relate to finances, which does not necessarily cover all humanitarian or development related activities of FBOs.

(Oxford Faith-Aligned Impact Finance Report, 2022)

Business and technology

The impact of international businesses is significant: they produce and provide what people need and want, ranging from electronics, energy, foodstuffs and pharmaceuticals to cars and tobacco. This production, however, is increasingly being questioned for its many downsides, in particular the negative impact on global health, consumerism, and climate change. To address these problems, it is argued that not only the producers but also the consumers need to make adjustments to, respectively, their production processes and lifestyles (see chapters 'Sustainable development' and 'Resources and Climate').

Non-state actors are also often responsible for the development of technology. The latest examples of such technology that have had an enormous impact globally are the internet, mobile phones, social media, space travel technology and Artificial Intelligence. However, the development of these technologies depends on the business environment in which they work that includes an educated work force, infrastructure, economic stability, and legal security. Such an environment is usually provided or at least guaranteed by the state. In other words, the non-states actors are the decisive factor in making this technological impact, but they cannot do so without the help of states. Similarly, once technological inventions have been made, it is the state that regulates their use.

Private international business impact

In his Space X program, private entrepreneur Elon Musk has developed space transport technologies that for the first time have become profitable. Elon Musk also owns hundreds of satellites that his organization has launched and controls. In 2022, he granted the Ukraine access to these satellites so that it could maintain communications during the war with Russia.

Private entrepreneur Bill Gates made his fortune as co-founder of the software company Microsoft and now has one of the largest charity funds in the world (with a capital of $75 billion in 2023) that focuses on education, poverty reduction and healthcare.

Crime and terrorism

The global impact of international crime and terrorist organizations is evident, but not easy to measure, also because they are different in nature, with varying interests. International **crime organizations** have financial interests, and since they are active in domains that are considered destructive to society – drugs, prostitution, human trafficking, weapons – the impact of their activities is usually exactly that: destructive to individuals and society. **Terrorist organizations**, on the other hand, pursue political interests. They usually identify themselves as resistance or liberation organizations, and use terrorist means to reach their goals. When they do so internationally – for instance, attacking their enemies in other states, or attacking states that support their enemies – these actions can have a global impact. The first hijackings of airplanes by Palestinians in the early 1970s, for instance, precipitated in a worldwide securitization of airports. In the 1970s, leftist extremist groups from across the world participated in joint training camps and so became a global menace. And the 2001 attacks by Al Qaeda on the United States led to a global 'War on Terror' with invasions of Afghanistan and Iraq. It was only after 2001 that terrorism was recognized as a global challenge (see chapter 'Security').

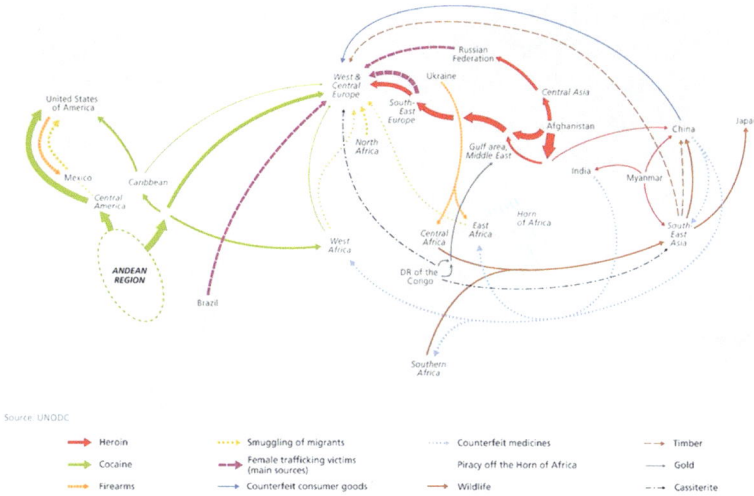

Figure II.4.1 Transnational organized crime

Criticism

Whether non-state actors are a blessing or a curse is debateable. In the case of international terrorist or criminal organizations, the verdict seems clear. In the case of international commercial corporations one can argue that they serve the needs of entire populations (to provide energy, basic materials, foodstuffs, consumer products, or employment) but one may question the means used to achieve these ends. In the past decades, the criticism of such corporations has increased.

Shell in Nigeria

Following a large oil spill in 2008, a group of Nigerians from Bodo, Ogoniland, launched a lawsuit against Shell in 2012. Shell agreed to pay £50 million in compensation after a Dutch court found the company partially liable for the Bodo oil spills. In 2021, a Milan court acquitted Shell for charges of corruption and bribery allegedly totalling $1.3 billion. In the same year, Shell paid $112 million as settlement with a Nigerian community over another oil spill.

But the criticism also extends to renowned non-state actors that engage in non-profit activities for humanitarian causes, like Oxfam, Amnesty, Greenpeace, or Feed the Children. The problem with these non-state actors, the critics say, is that they are self-righteous at best and elitist at worst, with little transparency or accountability. The criticism aimed at such altruistic organizations is therefore not aimed at their goals, but at the way these organizations are run: what gives them the authority to decide what needs to be done, and how truly independent are they? These criticisms are reminiscent of the image of the aristocratic elite of the old times – it may very well be that they act in the interest of the common good of the people, but they do so without transparency or accountability.

Criticism of NGOs expressed in mocking acronyms:
- GINGOs: government-controlled NGOs
- MANGOs: male-controlled NGOs
- BINGOs: business-controlled NGOs
- RINGOs: reactionary NGOs
- TINGOs: tribal-controlled NGOs

Further reading

Nicola Banks, David Hulme, Michael Edwards, "NGOs, States, and Donors Revisited: Still Too Close for Comfort?", *World Development*, Vol. 66, 2015, pp. 707-718

Ann M. Florini (ed.), *The Third Force: The Rise of Transnational Civil Society*, Carnegie Endowment for Interrnational Peace, 2000

Femida Handy, Jeffrey L. Brudney, Lucas C.P.M. Meijs (eds.), 'Faith-Based Organizations in Context' *Nonprofit and Voluntary Sector Quarterly*, Special edition, Vol.42, No.3, 2013

Hank Johnston, *What is a Social Movement?* Polity Pr, 2014

Mary Kaldor, *Global Civil Society: An Answer to War*, Wiley-Blackwell, 2003

Donatella della Porta and Mario Diani, *Social Movements: An Introduction*, Wiley-Blackwell, 2020 (3rd Edition)

Anita Ramasastry, "Corporate Social Responsibility Versus Business and Human Rights: Bridging the Gap Between Responsibility and Accountability" *Journal of Human Rights*, Vol. 14, No. 2, 2015, pp. 237-59

Jackie Smith and Dawn Wiest, *Social Movements in the World-System: The Politics of Crisis and Transformation*, Russel Sage Foundation, 2012

CHAPTER 5

Intergovernmental organizations

International organizations can be formed by non-state actors, as we saw in the previous chapter, but also by states. The latter can be grouped under the term intergovernmental organizations. They must be distinguished from alliances: an alliance is a temporary cooperation between parties, an international organization is a new entity established by several parties. Alliances are of all times, on the level of individuals, families, tribes, nations, and states. Intergovernmental organizations, on the other hand, are relatively new but have become one of the most pervasive global structures in the world today. States establish these organizations to achieve at least one of three goals: prosperity, peace, and the promotion of values. In terms of 3-Is, they therefore mostly pursue *interests*, in particular peace, security, and trade. A spin-off of these interests, however, is the pursuit of certain *ideas* (like free-market, human rights) and *identities* (pan-Islam, Pan-Africanism, European unity).

In this chapter, several types of intergovernmental organizations will be discussed whereby the main question is *why* they were established. What we will see with all these intergovernmental organizations is the dilemma of their founding states who, on the one hand, feel the need to establish such organizations but, on the other hand, are reluctant to give up their state sovereignty. The result is that most intergovernmental organizations are given little power to implement their decisions or policies, which reduces their effectiveness and autonomy.

> **International organization** is a general term for any organization that works on an international scale. **Intergovernmental organizations** are international organizations founded by states. **International non-governmental organizations** are international organizations founded by non-state actors.

International cooperation: the United Nations

As early as in the 1920s, immediately after the First World War, the initiative was taken to create a world platform where all states could come together to solve their differences. However, the League of Nations was unable to withstand the aggression of Japan in China and, later, Germany in Europe. The Second World War showed again the need for some kind of international platform for states to discuss issues of peace and conflict, and in 1945 the United Nations was established. The United Nations ran all the risks of being stillborn, just like its predecessor the League of Nations. However, two global situations arose that made the United Nations one of the most important players in international relations.

The first situation was the **Cold War** whereby the two hegemonic superpowers, the United States of America and the Soviet Union, perceived the other as an existential threat and, paradoxically, contained that threat by the doctrine of 'mutual assured destruction' (MAD). At the same time, they used all their persuasive powers to win over other states to their camp. This was what for the next decades would determine international relations. The United Nations, and especially its Security Council, was one of the few locations were the Americans and Soviets could meet and discuss their disputes. Also, in other conflicts the United Nations proved successful in diffusing some disputes that might otherwise have led to a full-blown war.

The second international issue that confronted the United Nations immediately after its foundation was the **process of de-colonization**. After the Second World War, the colonial empires started to crumble and as a result the United Nations, in the first two decades of its existence, expanded to include more than thirty new states that had gained their independence. This created tensions between the General Assembly, where these new states were voicing their anti-colonial criticism, and the Security Council where four of its five permanent members, France, the United Kingdom, the Soviet Union and America, had been (and in some instances still were) colonial powers. Paradoxically, in the 1950s and 1960s, America and the Soviet Union both proclaimed staunchly anti-colonialist policies, but these were mostly directed towards the British, French and Dutch colonies.

Organization of United Nations

The United Nations consists of two bodies: the Security Council and the General Assembly. The **General Assembly** represents all the member states, but their resolutions and declarations have no decisive power. That power belongs exclusively to the **Security Council**. This council has five permanent members (United States, Soviet Union, China, United Kingdom, France) and ten members that rotate with 2-year terms. Only the five permanent members have the **right of veto**.

The undemocratic set-up of the United Nations is questioned regularly, especially with the sharp increase of member states (from 51 states in 1945 to 193 states in 2024) and the emergence of new economic and political powers (India, Japan, Germany, Nigeria, South Africa, Brazil). An extra point of contention is that many of the new member states are former colonies of France and the United Kingdom who are both permanent member of the Security Council.

Regional political and economic cooperation: the European and African unions

It may seem perfectly logical for certain regions who share a historical, linguistic, and cultural legacy to cooperate in issues of trade, and perhaps even politics. It is interesting therefore that a European Union came into existence despite its multiple languages and cultures, while an Arab Union has never come about even though the more than twenty Arab countries share a language, history, and, to a certain extent, culture. This makes more pertinent the issue of 'why' such regional cooperation comes into existence. We will discuss this below using two examples, the European Union and the African Union.

European Union

After the devastating experiences of First World War (1914-1918) and the Second World War (1939-1945), the *raison d'être* of the European Union was the **prevention of war**. It was in this situation that the French minister of foreign affairs, Robert Schuman, who was from the German-speaking part of the French Elzas, formed a plan "to make war not only unthinkable but materially impossible." In 1951, Germany, France, and four other countries established the European Coal and Steel Community, in which they shared the coal and steel industry so that no country had exclusive access to these weapon-making resources. This European community was unique in the world because it was the first intergovernmental organization wherein states gave up sovereignty over these resources, and placed control of them outside its national authority. This is also known as supranationalism.

> **Supranationalism** means that an issue is elevated outside and above ('supra') the national state which gives up its right of say in this issue.

In 1975, the Coal and Steel Community was turned into the European Economic Community. The main goal was still to create a situation that would guarantee peace on the continent, but this new community also hoped to attain that goal by creating an **open market** whereby people and goods could freely move across borders. This single action accomplished two aims at once: it created prospects for a European economic prosperity, and it would build an interdependency among the member states so that they would benefit from each other rather than fight each other.

When the Soviet Union disintegrated after 1989, Eastern and Western Germany were joined to become the Germany that we know today. Allowing the union to take the place of a country that only half a century ago had drawn the continent into a devastating war shows how far the Europeans had come and how much trust there was among them. This spirit of togetherness also had its effect on the community itself. In 1992, a new transformation was made, and the European Economic Community became the European Union, a union that maintained its first two goals of preventing war and free movement of people and goods but now added a third goal as a **community of shared values**. However, these values, together with the rapid expansion of the Union, have created tensions among the member states. The large number of member states had increasing differences of views about the values they were supposed to share. Also, the system of taking decisions by consensus was harder to achieve with many than with few. And in several member states there was a growing opposition to the supranational character of the Union.

African Union

The reason for the founding of the Organization of African Unity in 1963 was decolonization: the entire African continent had been colonized by European powers, and most of these colonies obtained their independence in the 1950s and early 1960s. But the movements that had called for state independence had also called for some kind of African unity. This unity was known as **Pan-Africanism**, but although it was a notion that mobilized people, it was not entirely clear whether it referred to the unity of a shared past of colonialism, or a unity of a culture that was called Africa, or a more pragmatic unity of political or economic cooperation.

While acclaiming Pan-Africanism, all the new independent African states adhered to their separate **territorial and national unity**. However, many of these states, due to their colonial legacy, had little unity as a nation, since they upheld the colonial boundaries that cut through former tribal, territorial, cultural and linguistic boundaries. Nevertheless, territorial and national unity inherited from colonial times was strictly adhered to. Moreover, these states held a strong sense of **sovereignty**, and by consequence would not give any part of it up for some supranational organization, nor accept any interference from fellow-African states. The Organization of African Unity therefore became a loose association of independent and sovereign states. What remained of the ideal of Pan-Africanism was the objective to find African solutions for African problems, which was often more a slogan than an actively pursued objective.

This changed by the late 1990s. Two countries took the lead in reforming the Organization of African Unity: Nigeria, one of the most vibrant economies of the continent, and South Africa, that had just thrown off the system of apartheid and that had gained enormous prestige and authority in the continent. These two countries merged the concepts of good governance and human rights (based on the Organisation of Security and Cooperation in Europe) and a project called the 'African Renaissance' which focused on poverty reduction and sustainable development. In 2002, these initiatives led to a restructuring of the Organization of African Unity into the African Union. This Union still maintains as its main goal the 'common vision of united and strong Africa'. But this time the member states had given this

Union powers to reach that goal, including the right to intervene in cases of war crimes, genocide, crimes against humanity, and 'serious threats to the legitimate order'. This power of intervention is like that of the United Nations but goes much further than is, for instance, the case in the European Union. Since then, the African Union has summoned numerous military peace keeping missions to intervene in conflicts on the continent.

Faith-based state-organizations: Organization of Islamic Cooperation and Catholic Church

Among the international organizations are many that are based on faith. Most of these are non-state actors, as we have seen in the previous chapter, but there are two that have a distinct state-quality that deserves closer attention.

Intergovernmental organization based on faith: the Organization of Islamic Cooperation

The Organization of Islamic Cooperation (OIC) unites states with a Muslim majority population (and some with a Muslim minority population, like Surinam). What binds these states is not a region, like the European or African Union, or a purpose, like the United Nations, but a religion. However, the main reason for the OIC to be established in 1969 was the Israeli-Palestinian conflict. Apparently, this was considered an Islamic issue more than a political one.

The OIC had set itself three goals. The first was the **defense of Palestine**, but the organization failed to achieve any change or to play any significant role in the conflict. The OIC provided no material support nor did it initiate any diplomatic initiatives. The second goal was to promote **unity and cooperation** among its member states. The assumption was that the common bond of faith would generate shared interests. But this did not transpire, because even though the member states included such extremely wealthy countries as Saudi Arabia and Brunei, as well as extremely poor and developing countries like Bangladesh and Afghanistan, the solidarity among these states was apparently not enough to establish a system of sharing wealth and economic assistance.

The third goal was to create a **pan-Islamic identity**. This was perceived as a shared identity, and not as an ideology to unify the states. The charter of the OIC made clear that the member states enjoyed a sovereignty that was not to be violated nor surrendered to any supranational ideals. Nevertheless, it was in this identity that the member states found a common goal in the 1990s. In those years, criticism of Islam had become increasingly strong in Europe and in the United States. The OIC quite successfully used its diplomatic channels to put this issue on the international agenda: it introduced a resolution at the United Nations that called on the member states to prohibit the 'defamation of religion'. After years of deliberation, a compromise was reached: the OIC agreed that European countries did not need blasphemy laws to protect Islam, but the European countries would pledge themselves to jointly combat intolerance, discrimination, and violence that was based on religion.

Faith-based state with a transnational community: the Catholic Church

The Catholic Church has maintained organizational structures that date back more than a thousand years. At the same time, the Church has absorbed key elements of today's state and international organizations, making it a unique hybrid organization that is national as well as international and transnational (see chapter 'Transnationalism'). This shows in the following characteristics:

National: the place where the seat of this organization is established, Vatican City, is effectively a state, but with the special feature of being an absolute autocracy, with the Pope holding full legislative, executive, and judicial powers. This situation is not intentional but has grown historically. Vatican City State is not only functioning as a state but is also internationally recognized as such.

International: The Catholic Church has permanent observer status at the United Nations. This requires some explanation. Even though Vatican City is a recognized state, it never applied for membership of the UN. Instead, it preferred the status as permanent observer, which it got in 1964. Its full title was 'Non-Member State Permanent Observer' which is not a state like all the other states, but it is effectively treated like a state. The only other two entities that have such status are Switzerland (until it decided in 2002 to become a full member state) and Palestine since 2019.

Transnational: the Catholic Church represents a community of 1.2 billion believers all over the globe. This makes it the largest transnational organization in the world. The leader of the Church, the Pope, has an absolute say in what unites all these people: their faith.

Through all these organizational forms the Catholic Church has, in the words of Pope Francis (since 2013), one principal mission: 'evangelization, bringing the Good News to everyone'. The International Relations theorists therefore call the Catholic Church a '**norm entrepreneur**', that is. an actor who promotes certain norms.

> The Catholic Church maintains **two separate foreign relations**. One is political, by means of diplomats, also called nuncios, who are posted in other states (and those states also send their ambassadors to Vatican City). The other is religious, by means of bishops, who are also posted all over the world.

Other international purpose-oriented organizations

States have also established other types of organizations, mostly for specific purposes. Some of these organizations are intergovernmental, and some can be classified as alliances or as mere forums to meet. For instance, the United Nations has set up several intergovernmental agencies that are semi-independent and that work on specific issues, like the World Health Organization, the International Monetary Fund, and the Food and Agriculture Organization. States have also set up their own intergovernmental agencies for specific purposes, separate from the United Nations, like the World Bank (goal: 'reduce poverty'), NATO (goal: 'consult and cooperate on defence and security-related issues'), International Organization for Migration (goal: 'humane management of migration'), to name but a few. The degree of independence of these organizations from their founding states differs per organization.

Other intergovernmental forms of regional cooperation

ASEAN - Association of Southeast Asian Nations (10 member states): cooperation among states to "accelerate the economic growth, social progress and cultural development". No transfer of sovereignty: non-interference is explicitly agreed upon.

OAS - Organization of American States (34 member states): pursuit of four goals: democracy, human rights, security, and development. No transfer of sovereignty, but mutual accountability and transparency.

OSCE - Organization for Security and Cooperation in Europe (57 member states): Comprehensive approach to security, which also includes concerns about democracy, human rights, minorities, environment. Partial sovereignty transfer by means of the organization's ministerial council and parliament.

G-7: Forum where the 7 states with the world's largest economies (all Western) meet and discuss pressing issues. Sometimes the forum is extended to 20 states.

BRICS - Forum of emerging market economies that meets to discuss pressing issues. The forum is a political-economic response to the G-7. The acronym refers to the founding states: Brazil, Russia, India, China, South Africa. Since 2024, new member states are Saudi Arabia, Egypt, the United Arab Emirates, Iran, and Ethiopia.

Further reading

John Akokpari, Angela Ndinga-Muvumba, Tim Murithi (eds.), *The African Union and Its Institutions*, Jacana Media, 2009

Jacob Katz Cogan, Ian Hurd, Ian Johnstone (edss.), *The Oxford Handbook of International Organizations*, Oxford University Press, 2016

Akira Iriye, *Global Community. The Role of Internaitonal Organizations in the Making of the Contemporary World*, University of California Press, 2007

Stanley Meisler, *United Nations*, Grove Press, 2011

Luuk van Middelaar, *The Passage to Europe*, Yale University Press, 2013

Beth A. Simmons and Lisa L. Martin, "Chapter 10: International Organizations and Institutions" in *Handbook on International Relations*, Sage Publications, 2002

CHAPTER 6

International agreements

We have seen that states work together to achieve at least one of the following three goals: prosperity, peace, and the promotion of values. Some of the resulting organizations are so ambitious that they strive for all three goals, others attempt to achieve just one or two of them. The Church wants to promote peace and certain values related to human life, the African Union wants to achieve peace and prosperity, the United Nations and the European Union want all three. The way to do this is by agreement. Agreements among people are called contracts, among states they are called treaties, conventions, or charters. Treaties date back to the times that people organized themselves in communities and made agreements with other communities. Later, such treaties were signed between cities and states. Today, international treaties have become a new global structure.

> A **treaty** is concluded among two or more states. A **convention** is a treaty that states can sign up for (they then become 'member' to the convention). A **charter** is the rules and principles that an international or intergovernmental organization has set up for itself.

Why sign international treaties?

No state is forced to sign any treaty. So why would a state sign any treaty that will somehow limit its sovereignty? Ideally, because they expect that it will serve their interests. A peace treaty, or a treaty on the reduction of import tariffs does that. But in the case of a convention - that is a treaty offered to states in a region or the entire world to sign - there is also another reason: states want to be part of such a treaty because everyone else is. That treaty itself might perhaps not always be entirely beneficial for a state, but being part of the larger group of member states may serve the state's interests in the long run. The idea of an **international community** therefore hinges mostly on the psychology of belonging and peer pressure, which are elements that very few states can resist.

This phenomenon becomes particularly clear in human rights conventions (see also the chapter on 'Human Rights'). Some countries have signed very few, if any, such treaties, and they have become international pariahs, like North Korea. So was Sudan, until it signed most human treaties all at once in 2004 (a move that may be explained by the psychological factor of wanting to be part of the larger world community). Perhaps the most interesting example of those few who refuse to give up their sovereignty by signing human rights treaties is the United States of America. Its position is primarily motivated by the idea that it already has a functioning legal system that needs no additional treaties, but other considerations play a role as well (see text box).

Specific reasons why America has not signed human rights treaties

America had specific reasons to not sign the following international treaties:

- *International Criminal Court*: no American should be tried before a foreign court, including the embarrassing risk that an American president might be called before the court.
- *Convention on the Elimination of All Forms of Discrimination against Women (CEDAW)*: this would allow the right to abortion which is restricted in most, and fully banned in several American states.
- *Rights of Child*: the provision against child soldiers (under 18) would go against the practice of the American military to recruit soldiers at high school.
- *Optional Protocol to the Convention against Torture*: this treaty allows for inspection to detention facilities which America, with the largest incarcerated population in the world (2.3 million), considered 'overly intrusive'.

Treaties, particularly in the form of conventions, are a typical product of the global trend of multilateralism since the second half of the twentieth century: states were intent on cooperating and creating a world order by agreeing to abide by the same rules. It came therefore as a shock when the United States unilaterally withdrew from international treaties like the 2015 Joint Comprehensive Plan of Action (JCPOA) regarding Iran's nuclear program, the 2016 Paris Climate Accord that, among other points, sets standards for carbon dioxide emission reduction.

How to sign international treaties

When reference is made to states that have signed a treaty, a few legal-technical aspects need to be considered. First, there is a difference between a state 'signing' or 'ratifying' a treaty. **Signing** a treaty means that a government agrees with the treaty but still needs permission from parliament. A signed treaty is therefore not yet binding for that state. Once that permission is granted, the treaty can be **ratified** which means that the state is bound by it.

When a state ratifies a treaty, it can make reservations. A **reservation** means that a state ratifies a treaty but stipulates that some of the articles of the treaty are not applicable or need to be interpreted in a certain way. For example, America has ratified the International Convention for Cultural and Political Rights but made the reservation that the article prohibiting the death penalty for minors is not applicable. And several Muslim majority countries have ratified human rights treaties with the reservation that they only apply if they do not contradict the 'sharia'.

Has a state signed, ratified or made a reservation to a treaty?

To check the signatory status of states to treaties, one can peruse the online lists provided by the United Nations (https://treaties.un.org under 'Status of Treaties Deposited with the Secretary-General'). There, one can check for each state whether it has signed and/ or ratified the treaty and has possibly made any reservations.

Enforcing international treaties

Once certain rules and principles are agreed upon among states through a treaty, the question arises as to how the member states can be held to that treaty. Nationally, when a party breaks a contract, the other party can go to court to obtain a court order to have the contract enforced, and the court order will be enforced by the police. In the international community of states there is no such mechanism of enforcement: there are very few international courts (see next paragraph), and those that exist often have limited mandates. But more importantly: there is no international police. Therefore, a system has been created whereby states can hold each other accountable.

One of the ways to do so is **annual reporting**. During annual meetings, treaty member states assemble to report how they are upholding the treaty and to criticize each other for violations of that treaty. Accusing other states for not upholding the principles that they signed up for has no repercussions other than an international loss of face. This is a subtle way of public shaming and blaming and shows the psychology and diplomacy of international interactions.

A second option of enforcement is the deployment of **military force**. This option has been used in numerous instances by intergovernmental organizations like the United Nations, the African Union and NATO. It must be noted that the United Nations has no army, but the Security Council may decide that military force is permitted in a particular situation. The African Union and NATO, both of which can instruct member states to use their armies, will only do so upon the permission ('mandate') of the United Nations. This international use of military force has marked a change in the use of national armies: their function is now not only to defend their own country but may also be to defend peace elsewhere in the world. However, the deployment of such international defense forces is often questioned because of the limited mandates that they are given by the intergovernmental organization that deploys them. Usually, their presence merely serves as a buffer between warring parties, and military force is only allowed as a measure of self-defense, which severely limits the options to use force (see chapter 'Security'). Only a few times have international forces been given the mandate to exercise military aggression, like in the case of North-Korea (1950-1953) and Iraq (1990-1991, and 2003).

> **NATO's Article 5**
> According to Article 5 of the NATO treaty, all member states are required to come to the defense of another member state if that state is being attacked.

Another way to enforce treaties is through **international courts**. Several of the international and regional organizations have given supranational powers to international courts to adjudicate in matters that are defined by the charters of these same organizations. The first such court is the International Court of Justice, mandated by the United Nations to adjudicate between member states based on **international law** (which is based on the amalgam of treaties, UN resolutions, and international practices). This Court has been mainly used in border conflicts between states, but also in matters of war (Nicaragua-United States in 1984, Congo-Uganda in 1999, Ukraine-Russia in 2014 and 2022), apartheid (South Africa in 1960, Israel in 2024) and genocide (Serbia in 2015, Myanmar in 2020, Israel in 2024). Another international court established by the United Nations is the International Criminal Court, that does not prosecute states but only individuals who are accused of crimes against humanity. Sometimes, the United Nations has set up ad hoc courts, like the Khmer Rouge Tribunal in Cambodia, the International Criminal Tribunal for the Former Yugoslavia, or the Special Tribunal for Lebanon.

Regional organizations may also install courts to adjudicate on matters relating to the charter of the organization. This is the case with the Court of Justice for the European Union, and the Court of Justice for the African Union. Sometimes a regional organization may install a court that only deals with issues of **human rights**, such as the Inter-American Court of Human Rights, the European Court of Human Rights, the African Court on Human and Peoples' Rights. In all these instances the states that established these courts have been willing to submit part of their judicial sovereignty to these courts. Sometimes it was the logical thing to do because the court was meant to adjudicate in conflicts among members of an intergovernmental organization or to explain legal points of its charter. But sometimes it was a principal decision to subject certain domains of law – in particular human rights – to a supranational court.

The thorny issue with international courts is the enforcement of their rulings. If the proceedings involve individuals, as is the case with human rights and international criminal courts, the enforcement of those rulings is undertaken by the countries of the convicted person (except in the case of the International Criminal Court in The Hague which has the use of its own prison). In court rulings among states, which is the mandate of the International Court of Justice, there is no enforcement mechanism, and there are cases known where the convicted state refused to implement the ruling, and the international community did not have the will or means to enforce it.

Further reading

Emmanuelle Tourme Jouannet, *A Short Introduction to International Law*, Cambridge University Press, 2015

Avidan Kent, Nikos Skoutaris, Jamie Trinidad (eds.), *The Future of International Courts. Regional, Institutional and Procedural Challenges*, Routledge, 2019

George Lawson, "The Rise of Modern International Order", in: Baylis, John, Smithson, Steve and Owens, Patricia, (eds.) *The Globalization of World Politics: An Introduction to International Relations*, Oxford University Press, 2016, pp. 37-51

Hanns W. Maull (ed.), *The Rise and Decline of the Post-Cold War International Order*, Oxford University Press, 2018

Cecily Rosen, *et al.*, *An Introduction to Public International Law*, Leiden University, Press 2022

Dinah Shelton, "Form, Function, and the Powers of International Courts," *Chicago Journal of International Law*: Vol. 9: No. 2, 2009, pp.1-29

CHAPTER 7

Migration

Migration is as old as humankind: people have always moved, either because they were forced to do so by wars, hunger, or natural calamities, or because they sought a better place to live. As such, migration can be considered a global structure.

The issue of definitions

Migration is usually defined as the movement of persons away from their habitual place of residence to another place which can be in the same country or elsewhere. This movement can be temporary or permanent. While this definition would, strictly speaking, also include tourism and pilgrimage, these two forms of human movement are usually excluded from the discussion on migration.

> **Migration** is usually defined as the movement of people to another place where they reside at least twelve months. **International** migration is a movement that crosses at least one border. **Domestic** (also: **internal**) migration takes place within a single country. '**Emigration**' is a term often used for people moving out of a country, '**immigration**' for people who move into a country.

Average number of annual pilgrims (in millions):

India:	Hindu Mela (Hindu)	10-70
India:	Ayyappan Saranam, (Hindu)	30
Mexico:	Lady of Guadalupe (Catholic)	20
Brazil:	Our Lady of Aparecida (Catholic)	15
Iraq:	Karbala (Shi'ite Muslim)	10
France:	Lourdes (Catholic)	6
Portugal:	Fátima (Catholic)	4-5
Israel:	Wailing Wall (Jewish)	4-5
Nigeria:	Qadiriyyah shrine (Muslim)	3
China:	Wutai Shan (Daoist)	2
Saudi-Arabia:	Mecca (Muslim)	2

This definition of migration is descriptive and must be distinguished from legal or political definitions. For example, the term 'migrant' has no status under international law as opposed, for instance, to the notions of 'refugee' or 'migrant worker' that are specific types of migrants as defined in international treaties. Similarly, it is common for international organizations to use the term 'labor migration', while the notions of 'economic refugee', 'economic migrant', 'undocumented migrant', or 'irregular migration' are mostly used in national political and public discourse, often with the implication of illegality.

In this chapter, we will use the descriptive and legal terminology as used by international organizations: the political terminology will be discussed in the chapter 'Unwanted migration'. Still, occasional confusion will arise when using this terminology because it often refers to the specific frameworks of these organizations and treaties and is subject to the goals they pursue. The International Organization of Migration (IOM), the International Labour Organization (ILO), and the United Nations High Commissioner for Refugees (UNHCR) may serve as examples. The UNHCR only uses statistics of refugees who are registered with the UNCHR. Their use of the term 'refugee' is based on the International Refugee Treaty that defines such person as someone who flees conflicts or persecution. The IOM, on the other hand, uses a much wider definition of the migrant as 'a person who moves away from his or her place of usual residence, whether within a country or across an international border, temporarily or permanently, and for a variety of reasons.' Since the 2010s, both organizations have identified climate change as a source of 'forced migration' and are developing strategies to address this issue. For the IOM this means an expansion of practical projects, for the UNHCR it may mean an expansion of the number of 'refugees' who are entitled to legal support. Another source of confusion in terminology is the notion of 'migrant workers'. When the IOM and ILO use this notion, it is commonly meant as a type of voluntary migration. Moreover, these organizations usually focus on the 'legal' labor migration, that is migrant workers who have permission to work in another country. However, there are many politicians who are worried about the 'illegal' (or: 'undocumented') migrants (see chapter Unwanted Migration). The numbers of this latter category of migrants are subject to speculation since they are not registered and therefore cannot be easily determined.

Why migration?

A distinction is usually made between voluntary and forced migration. **Voluntary migration** is triggered by 'pull factors', that is factors of a place that attract people to move there, examples of this would be study, work, or better living conditions. **Forced migration** (also: 'displacement') is triggered by 'push factors', that is, factors at the place of residence that make life so unbearable that people are coerced to leave. Examples are war, calamities, famine, drought, poverty. Of course, this typology is not always accurate. 'Voluntary' migration may be considered a misnomer if we consider that people in general do not want to leave, unless their living situations are considered difficult or untenable. The 'voluntary' motivations to migrate can therefore differ widely, ranging from Western European farmers who migrate to countries like Ukraine or Kenya to escape stringent legal regulations in their country of origin, to people who move to Europe to escape dire poverty. In both cases of voluntary and forced migration, the reason for migration can be viewed as a combination of escaping a specific situation and a pursuit of better opportunities. However, since the terminology of voluntary and forced migration has become common parlance in national and international politics, and therefore also in most academic literature, it will be the terminology used in this chapter.

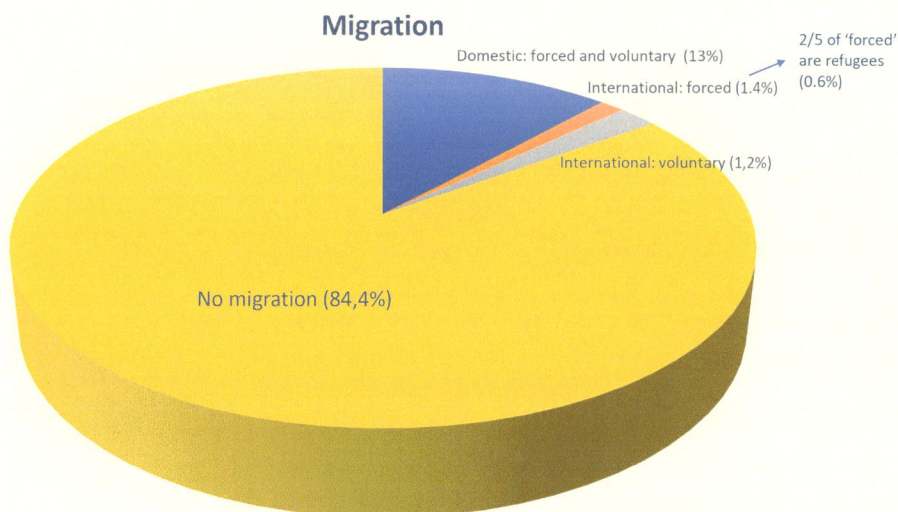

Figure II.7.1 Migration in the world

A form of forced migration that took place on a large scale in the past but has been formally abolished today is **slavery**. Capturing people and selling them into slavery was widely practiced almost everywhere in the world for thousands of years, resulting in moving the enslaved peoples away from their place of origin. One of the latest examples of such massive deportations was the trans-Atlantic transport of African people into slavery in America. While slavery has been abolished and is forbidden by all countries in the world, hidden forms of it still exist.

Forced migration (or: displacement) worldwide (2024 statistics)

Total: 117 million

Domestic:	68-71 million
International:	
refugees:	35-38 million
asylum-seekers:	5.5-7 million
'Others':	5-6 million

Of these forced migrants:

73% from following countries:		39% hosted in following countries:	
- Afghanistan:	6.4 million	- Iran:	3.8 million
- Syria:	6.4 million	- Türkiye:	3.3 million
- Venezuela:	6.1 million	- Columbia:	2.9 million
- Ukraine:	6.0 million	- Germany:	2.6 million
- South Sudan:	2.3 million	- Pakistan:	2.0 million

(IOM and UNHCR, 2024)

Modern slavery

According to the International Labour Organization (ILO) and the International Organization for Migration (IOM), an estimated 50 million people were living in **'modern slavery'** worldwide in 2021. This group of people consists of 28 million in forced labor and 22 million trapped in forced marriage.

(ILO, *Global Estimates of Modern Slavery*, 2024).

Academic researchers have indicated that **human trafficking** is mostly persistent in various (often serious) forms of labor exploitation, but is hardly ever of the same nature as slavery.

(Hein de Haas, Stephen Castles, Mark J. Miller, *The Age of Migration*, 2023.)

Whereto migration?

The main part of today's migration is domestic, that is migration that does not cross borders but remains within the country. This type of migration predominantly moves from the countryside to the large cities (a process also known as **urbanization**), but some of it is forced migration because of war, famine or natural disasters. Domestic migrants make up approximately 60 percent of all known migration and 13 percent of the world population.

Urbanization

In 2016, half of the world's population lived in cities. By 2030, it is estimated that 60 per cent of people globally will live in cities, and of these, one in every three people will live in cities with at least half a million inhabitants.

(UN-Habitat, *World Cities Report 2016*)

Most (political) focus, however, is on international migrants (approximately 3.6 percent of the world population) and even more so on refugees (approximately 0.3 percent of the world population). Of the international migration, an estimated one-third is considered forced migration and two-thirds is voluntary (often also called 'labor') migration. Voluntary migration today is directed towards America and Europe, and recently also towards the fast-growing economies in the Arab Gulf and in South-East Asia. It must be kept in mind that these are the known ('registered') numbers and that the estimates of undocumented migrants are unknown and therefore prone to speculation.

International migration destinations

1. USA
2. Germany
3. Saudi Arabia
4. Russia
5. United Kingdom
6. United Arab Emirates
7. Canada / France
8. Australia
9. Spain / Italy
10. Turkey

(IOM, *World Migration Report*, 2024)

Effects of migration

The effects of migration are manifold, depending on the type of migration and on the perspective of the place of departure or arrival. Domestic migration, for instance, has **depopulated** rural areas and in hot areas sometimes even contributed to desertification because the agricultural lands left un-maintained. As regards the point of arrival (mostly the city), domestic migration has resulted in rapid expansion of these cities, sometimes even developing into mega-cities. While migration to the city is usually referred to as **urbanization**, a large influx of people from rural areas may have the effect of **ruralization** on city life, meaning that certain traditions and values from the countryside may impact urban traditions and values. (In some Western countries the term 'ruralization' is now also used to refer to the gradual movement of well-to-do people from the city to the countryside.)

Mega-cities

A mega-city is usually defined as a city with more than 10 million inhabitants. They are considered future global challenges because of their unique issues on an environmental, governmental, migratory, social and political level. The largest mega-cities are:

Tokyo (Japan):   37 million
Jakarta (Indonesia):   35 million
Delhi (India):   32 million
Guangzhou (China):   27 million
Seoul (South Korea):   26 million

In some instances, migration may lead to a '**brain drain**': the high-skilled people that have little opportunity in their own country, either because the pay is low or because there is no employment for high-skilled labor, may decide to move to countries where such skills are needed. As a result, the country of origin may become depleted of the knowledge and skills that are needed to develop the technological and economic infrastructures of those countries

Migrant workers who move abroad to find work often do so with the purpose of sending money back to their families in the country of origin. These so-called **remittances** may amount to significant sources of income for those countries. The statistics show that labor migration does not originate in poorer countries only: people from relatively rich countries, like France, may also take on jobs abroad and send their money home (see infogram).

Migration may can have an impact on the **demographics** in the country of arrival. This may be considered a problem if it causes a population to grow significantly (which is almost never the case), but from a demographic point of view it may be considered beneficial for countries with an aging population. If the birth rate is so low that there are more elderly people than young, a society runs the risk that there are too few people to sustain the population. It has been argued that a demographic 'injection' from abroad may bring the demographics back into balance.

> **Remittances**
>
> The total sum of remittances in 2023 was estimated between US$ 669 and 831 billion[*].
> The top remittance recipients in that year were:
>
> India: $125 billion
> Mexico: $67 billion
> China: $50 billion
> Philippines: $40 billion
> France: $34 billion
>
> [*] World Bank, *Migration and Development Brief No.39*, 2023 lists US$ 669 billion, while the IOM, *World Migration Report 2024* lists US$ 831 billion

Migration may also have an impact on the society of arrival from a **socio-cultural** point of view. When the numbers of migrants are significant, the receiving society may perceive it as a threat to its social and cultural identity and values. This is mostly the case in Western countries, and it is one of the major reasons that in these countries migration is considered one of the main challenges that their societies are facing (for further discussion, see chapter 'Unwanted Migration').

The individual dimension of migration

Migration is usually discussed in relation to mass movements and, therefore, in numbers and statistics. Consequently, migration is addressed as a matter of policy by states and international organizations and as a type of social movements by scholars. The individual migrant receives very little, if any attention. In everyday life, however, many people are dealing daily with individual migrants as people who have left their country of origin or are settling in the country of destination, just as these individual migrants are balancing the connection with their home and host countries (see chapter 'Transnationalism'). These experiences are individual and therefore very diverse but may lead to generalizations in public and political discourses when the migration is significant in numbers. The few instances that migration is being individualized is when news media provide background stories about migration, or when organizations want to raise awareness of migration issues: in these instances, usually the stories and images of individual migrants are being used. Such images and stories can be informative, but also a way to frame the discussion and perception of migration, just as the critics of migration may use images of masses of people to amplify the impression of migration as mass movement that threatens the destination country.

What to call the migrant after arrival?

Destination countries use terms like 'refugee', 'immigrant', 'foreigner', 'alien'. The motives for these terms may differ for legal or policy reasons, but they all have in common that they make a distinction between the 'national' and the 'other'. Some countries feel the need to continue making the distinction between 'migrants' and 'native population' when it regards the next generations that are born and raised in that country and have the nationality of that country. Academics must therefore beware of the terminology they use: do they refer to the country's official vocabulary, or the terminology that is commonly used in that society, or can they find a neutral and descriptive term?

Further reading

David Bartram, Maritsa V. Poros & Pierre Monforte, *Key Concepts in Migration*, Sage Publications, 2017

Stephen Castles and Mark J. Miller, *The Age of Migration. International Population Movements in the Modern World*, Red Globe Press, 1998

James F. Hollifield and Neil Fole (eds.), *Understanding Global Migration*, Stanford University Press, 2022

Elizabeth Mavroudi and Caroline Nagel, *Global Migration: Patterns, Processes and Politics*, Routledge, 2023 (2nd edition)

PART III
Global Trends

In this textbook, 'global trend' is defined as a manner of thinking or behaving that gains worldwide recognition or imitation. In the following chapters we will discuss seven important global trends that still affect the world today. Some of these trends have a political impact, while others are more important in the academic domain where they provide new outlooks on human behavior. What distinguishes global trends from global structures is that the trends represent recent developments that have not yet consolidated into global structures, that have faded away before ever becoming a global structure, or that have evolved into something else. For instance, some argue that the global trend of secularization that was dominant in the second half of the twentieth century is being replaced by a new trend of increasing religionization, while others argue that religion has always been a global structure and that the secularism of the twentieth century was merely a glitch in history. Another example is the global trend of international cooperation, which appeared to become a global trend in the second half of the twentieth century, but since the 2010s is being challenged by an emerging unilateralism.

CHAPTER 1

Power changes

The exercise of power is an intricate part of human nature and as such may be considered a global structure. However, in the second half of the twentieth century, we can observe two trends related to power: one relates to the international practice of power, the other to the way we think about power.

International practices of power

Since the Second World War, the world has witnessed a decrease in the number of wars between states and an increase of cooperation among states resulting in a proliferation of international organizations. It seemed that a large part of the world had moved from power and prestige to peace and cooperation. To some, this development heralded the emergence of a new global structure (or, as some preferred to call it: a "new world order"). To others, these processes merely represented a temporary phase in the history of humankind pointing out a continuation of power politics by states like America, Russia and China, and the re-emergence of unilateral actions by these states since the 2010s. The latter raises the question whether international cooperation is a global trend that will consolidate into a global structure or is merely a global trend that is fading away. Since we are in the middle of these developments, we cannot conclude on the outcome yet: have we indeed moved from power and prestige to peace and cooperation, or has this development been reversed since the 2010s?

Whatever the case, it is a development that we can call a global trend, regardless of whether it will develop in a global structure or is about to end. To analyze this trend, we will use two frames of reference: power and leadership. Both frames are fueled by the 3-Is (Interests, Ideas, and Identities). When the 3-Is energize people, power is a means to use this energy, and leadership is a means to channel that power. It is then the leader's choice to wield that power alone (unilateralism) or to cooperate with others (multilateralism). These three elements – power, leadership, and uni- or multilateralism – are key to understanding the developments that are taking place in the global trend of international cooperation and will be discussed below.

Power

One way of looking at power is the ability to influence the behavior or thinking of others to arrive at a desired outcome. In short: the ability to make others do what you want them to do. Defined this way, power is present in almost every human interaction, from raising children to landing jobs to running companies and waging wars.

The next question is how that power is wielded. In the interaction among states, we often distinguish between **'hard' and 'soft' power**, that is between the power to coerce and the power to convince, respectively. These notions also apply to interhuman relations. While for centuries was considered a measure of power that earned respect – think of kings leading their men into battle – seemed to have become the new trend in second half of the twentieth century. The battle-hardened warrior was replaced by the well-spoken orator. Both have the same aim – creating order – but seek to reach it with different means. To many, soft power appeared to be a new global trend.

Language is power…

'Each society has its regime of truth, its "general politics" of truth: that is, the types of discourse which it accepts and makes function as true; the mechanisms and instances which enable one to distinguish true and false statements, the means by which each is sanctioned; the techniques and procedures accorded value in the acquisition of truth; the status of those who are charged with saying what counts as true'

(Michel Foucault, in Paul Rabinow (ed.) *The Foucault Reader: An introduction to Foucault's thought*, 1991)

However, critics have pointed out that the exercise of soft power is subject to other, internal power dynamics. They believe power is not only what people do or say, it is also embedded in who they are. In interactions among people, for instance, structures of patriarchy, religion or racism often still play a role. A woman may be the minister and therefore holding a position of power, but that power can be undercut by people who consider the fact that she is a woman a disadvantage to that position of power. Similar power plays are waged in cases involving people from different color, social background and religion, amongst others. The power imbalances at the foundation of these occurrences also manifest themselves at the level of states: former colonized countries are still very sensitive to a condescending tone or treatment from their former colonizer, just as the colonizer may still have difficulty to kick that habit, possibly out of an enduring belief in its superiority.

Since the 2010s, a new dimension of power has emerged in these power dynamics which can be considered 'manipulation'. This is referred to as **'sharp power'** which taps into the omnipresent information technology that can be manipulated into, and is conducive to the production of fake news and disinformation to influence people. But sharp power is not just another form of soft power; it can also take the shape of hard power when the manipulation of information takes on aggressive forms by means of hacks, deep fakes, possibly state-driven. Examples may include state-run 'troll farms' that target certain information sources with disruptive forms of disinformation, or states investing in foreign information and knowledge sectors like universities or social media, to manipulate information flows in foreign countries. Sharp power has grown exponentially with the development of digital technology.

> **Power** is the ability to influence the behaviour or thinking of others by means of coercion (**hard power**), convincing (**soft power**) or manipulation (**sharp power**).

Leadership

Leadership is traditionally connected to hard power, as demonstrated by the notion of the warrior-king that still resonates in the image that some of today's leaders like to portray. But what did leadership look like during the global trend that replaced power and prestige with peace and cooperation?

Leadership has been a topic of research in Humanities for a long time, and a helpful analysis has been provided by one of the founding fathers of sociology, Max Weber (d. 1920). According to him, a key notion to understand leadership is **authority**. He argues that authority is based on the belief that people have about the legitimacy of a person's authority. He then distinguishes three types of authority: **traditional authority** is based on the belief in the sanctity of immemorial traditions (examples are hereditary royalty, whether as clan chiefs, kings or emperors); **legal authority** is based on the belief of the legality of rules according to which a person is appointed in an authoritative role (like the elected president, the appointed professor or judge); **charismatic authority** is based on the devotion to exceptional qualities of the individual person (e.g., Hitler, Napoleon, Ghandi, Mandela). Ideally, these three types will overlap, as has been the case with some popes: their authority is enshrined in traditions that go back for almost nineteen centuries, while each pope is elected according to a strict procedure, and some popes enjoy charismatic qualities due to their character or policies.

> **Traditional and legal authority in Asia**
>
> In the second half of the twentieth century, Asian countries have seen quite some instances where female prime ministers and presidents were elected who were the daughters or spouses of male leaders of their countries, thereby combining hereditary and legal authority: Benazir Bhutto of Pakistan, Indira Ghandi of India, Sirimavo Bandaranaike of Sri Lanka, Megawati Sukarnoputri of Indonesia, Khaleda Zia and Sheikh Hasina Wazed of Bangladesh, Corazon Aquino of the Philippines, Park Geun-hye of South Korea, Aung San Suu Kyi of Myanmar.

Figure III.1
Martial leadership

Vladimir Putin (Russia)   *Kim Jong-Un (North Korea)*

Margaret Thatcher (United Kingdom)   *George W. Bush (United States)*

Another element of authority that Weber points out, is the context, or the moment in history in which the authority is displayed. For instance, Churchill was very unpopular in pre-war times because of his hard-power rhetoric, but he rose to the occasion during the Second World War, only to be voted out of office immediately after the war. Simply put: 'hard' times seem to require hard-power leaders while times of peace and rebuilding require soft-power leaders. This may explain the dominance of soft power during the second half of the twentieth century: most Western states were recovering from a devastating world war while the former colonies were gaining independence and were building their own states. Hard power was not absent, however: the Cold War led to numerous proxy wars where 'communist' forces backed by the Soviet-Union were pitted against 'liberal' and autocratic forces backed by the United States, just like the process of de-colonization in some instances was forced by wars, and the establishment of new states out of former colonies often resulted in autocratic regimes trying to bend these new states to their will.

> The philosopher Joseph Raz distinguishes between two kinds of authority. **'Normal'**
> **authority** is when people accept someone's authority because it is in their interest.
> **'Deviant' authority** is when one feels obligated to obey, like deference to one's parents
> or by ideas like nationalism or religion.
> (Joseph Raz, *Authority*, 1990)

Multi- and unilateralism

During the second half of the twentieth century, international cooperation
prevailed. These decades were dominated by leaders who favored cooperation and
negotiation with an international focus. They adopted a **multilateral** approach,
seeing benefit in international cooperation. The number and types of international
treaties were unprecedented. But while many leaders may have aspired to world
peace, the goal of the multilateral approach ultimately remained national: only
through multilateralism could conflicts about trade, values, and the use of resources
be prevented and, consequently, the national interests be safeguarded. Since the
second decade of the 21st century, however, we have been observing an increase
in popularity of leaders who are tough, less diplomatic, and with an exclusively
national focus. They resort to a **unilateral** approach, meaning that they see no
benefit in international cooperation to promote national interests. (For the resulting
global trend – and to some: global challenge – of 'multipolarization' that is taking
place since the 2010s, see chapter 'Post-colonialism and decolonization'.)

> **Multilateralism** refers to two states or more communicating in the pursuit of their
> interests. **Unilateralism** refers to the preference of a state to pursue its interests
> without consulting, agreeing or cooperating with other states.

The reasons for the unilateral approach can be found in the 3-Is and appear to be
two-fold. On the one hand, the sentiment held by these leaders is that the results
of international cooperation are not enhancing but limiting the national *interests*.
This was one of the main reasons for the decision of the United Kingdom to leave
the European Union in 2020: while there were plenty of benefits from being part of
this regional organization, it was considered better to be able to make decisions
without the influence of European rules. Whereas this motivation for unilateralists
is related to interests, the other motivation is about *identity*: the unilateralists feel
that internationalization and globalization is contaminating their national identity,
and they therefore resort to politics of defending and restoring that identity.

In either case, unilateralists feel the need to detach themselves from multilateral
obligations so that they can set a national agenda in accordance with their own
wishes. As a result, we can observe the debate about states rescinding their

membership from international organizations and agreements increase. Also, we can see an increasing popularity of *hard power*, unrestrained by international customary rules or agreements.

The way we think about power

In addition to this shifting trend in the international practice of power, the second half of the twentieth century also gave rise to a new way of thinking about power. This manifested mostly in academic circles. The academic approach of considering people as part of a social, cultural, religious or ethnic group, was gradually replaced by the new point of view that these groups were not fixed social categories but flexible social relations. In other words: these groups were the product of social relations, and they also produced social relations themselves. For example, it only makes sense to talk about a social underclass if there is a social upper class, just like it only makes sense to talk about men if there are women, or the religious if there is a secular. These social positions are considered not to be static, but subject to relations of power. For that reason, the term 'slave' has been replaced by 'enslaved', to indicate that it is a social situation that can only occur if somebody is doing the enslaving and that the status of slavery is not a matter of choice for those who are subjected to it.

This way of viewing relations between people has become dominant since the late twentieth century, both in the academic and in the political domain. An important consequence is that certain social and political situations are not considered static or self-evident, such as the dominant position of the West, the patriarchy or the authority of the clergy, but that they are products of power relations. That means that such relations do not need to be accepted as fixed but can be challenged. Whereas opposition to power relations is of course not new and humankind has a long history of challenging those in power, what has shifted is that these power relations are no longer considered in terms of *groups* of fixed social status (women, laborers, the enslaved) who revolt against their oppressor, but as relations that *individuals* have with their social environment. This view allows for more realism when describing social situations but also creates more complexity. For instance, the laborer who protests the abuses of his employer may very well find it natural that his wife should obey him and that he should abide by the counsel of the local priest. Just like a former colony can still suffer from the continued political and economic power exercised by the former colonizer and at the same time maintain a harsh security apparatus and outlaw homosexuality. (See also Chapters 'Equality' and 'Identity').

Further reading

Michel Foucault, *Power. Essential Works 1954-1984*, Penguin Classics, 2020

Joseph S. Nye, *The Future of Power*, Public Affairs, 2011

Joseph Raz, *Authority*, NYU Press, 1990

Mario Telò, *Multilateralism Past, Present and Future: A European Perspective*, Routledge, 2023

Christopher Walk and Jessica Ludwig, *From 'Soft Power' to 'Sharp Power'. Rising Authoritarian Influence in the Democratic World* (report), National Endowment for Democracy, 2017

CHAPTER 2

Identity

Identity is not fixed, it is what people name themselves or others. The process of identifying is often one of binary opposites: civilized versus barbarian, man versus woman, believer versus non-believer, city versus countryside dweller, local versus foreign. Such identification may carry social, political and legal qualifications because it implies that people have a different status and different rights. As a result, identification can also be intended to indicate another binary: superiority versus inferiority.

'Othering'

One way of identifying one-self is by opposing one's identity to the identity of others: us-them, black-white, civilized-barbaric, male-female, sane-sick, native-foreign. This process is called Othering. Such binaries are sometimes made for a lack of clear self-definition, but sometimes also to claim superiority towards the 'other'.

While we may refer to identity and identification as a global structure, it's also subject to global trends. For instance, from the 1950s through the 1970s, it was common to identify people in terms of class. This was a Marxist concept to analyze people's needs and predicaments, and to describe the political and social relations on a national and global scale. Looking at humankind through the lens of class determined how governments made policy, how history was studied, how people regarded each other. For instance, some states made a point of including different 'classes' of the population – like 'laborers' or 'women' – in their parliamentarian representation by allotting them a reserved number of seats. Starting in the 1990s, however, this lens of class identity was replaced by identities like race, religion, gender. As a result, attention to and interest in social and economic class differentiations in society has diminished, even though these differentiations are still very much existent.

Marxist class theory: the history of the Haitian independence war

In his seminal study *The Black Jacobins* from 1938, the black historian C.L. James from Trinidad describes the causes and developments of the slave revolt of Haiti which resulted in the independence of that country. His description and analysis of the colonial oppression on Haiti is entirely framed in (Marxist) terms of property and class, and hardly refers to the issue of race.

From the 1990s onwards, we observe two new global trends in identity and identification that take place across the 3-D chessboard of human interactions. On a local, national, and global level there is the emergence of so-called identity politics. On a social and academic level we can observe the increasing popularity of understanding human relations in terms of individual identity. We will discuss both below.

Identity politics

Since the 1980s, politicians and states, but also people in general, have shown an increasing tendency to label their societies with a distinct identity that goes beyond the average self-awareness of any nation. Mostly these are religious identities: Hindu nationalism in India, Islam as a state identity in various countries with a Muslim-majority, Judeo-Christian civilization in European countries, or the exact opposite by identifying with non-religion, as is the case with secularism in France. Others are social-cultural: Nordic culture in Scandinavian societies, African culture in African countries, the revival of various native cultures around the world, to name but a few examples.

To some observers, these identifications are not trends but innate to underlying civilizations. The political scientist Samuel Huntington elaborated this idea in the 1990s and developed it into a world map of civilizations that he labelled mostly with religious identities (Confucian, Islamic, Hindu, Slavic-Orthodox) and partly with geographical-cultural identities (Western, Japanese, Latin American, African). His use of different identity markers – geographic and religious – was criticized by quite some scholar (what, then, are the criteria of a 'civilization'?), but what generated most discussion was Huntington's assertion that the identity differences between these civilizations would cause global conflicts.

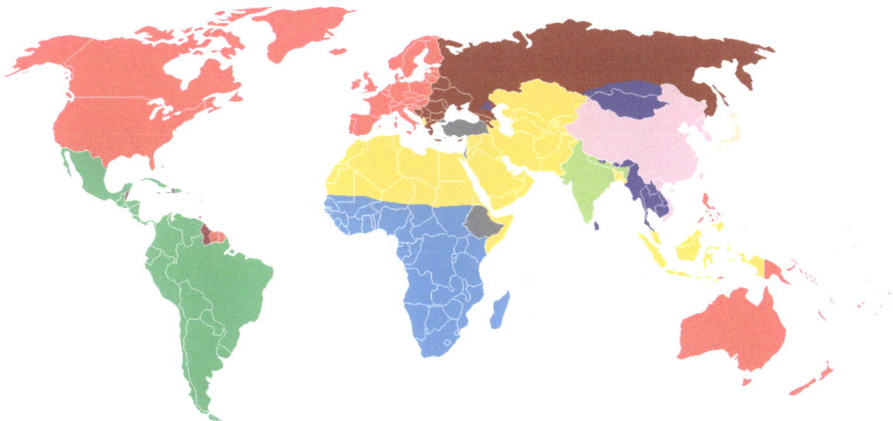

Figure III.2.1 Huntingtons' classification of 'civilizations'

However, what Huntington was predicting seemed to reflect the reality on the ground: many states and people had started to identifiy themselves in categories that went beyond the identity of the community, the nation or the state. This created new and, arguably, imaginary realms or regions in which people felt bonded through a particular identity. And yes, these realms also entailed a sentiment of conflict. For instance, the notion of a 'Judeo-Christian' culture as invoked by several politicians and political parties in European countries was mostly intended to counter the perceived corruption of domestic cultures by foreign cultures (particularly Islam) introduced by immigrants. In countries with a Muslim majority, the identification with Islam has caused tensions with non-Muslim minority communities, sometimes on a national level in the form of Islamic legislation that discriminates non-Muslims, sometimes on a local level by Muslims who, emboldened by the pronounced Islamic identity of their state, started to harass non-Muslims. A similar development is taking place in India, where the government of the Hindu national party contributed to already existing tensions between the Hindu majority and the Muslim minority. And in Russia, the self-identification of a greater Russia with Orthodox roots entailed the reclaiming of former empirical territories, and was one of the justifications to invade Ukraine in 2022.

The question is whether these processes are a cause or effect. Is identity inherently part of regional 'civilizations' and are these identities now being abused, causing tensions and even violence? This is what Huntington claims, arguing that such civilizations and their clashes are global structures. Another view, however, holds that these processes are a recent global trend, in other words self-identification is a recent phenomenon that has contributed to the establishment of regional identities. Regardless of the correct explanation of these developments, we are witnessing the increasing popularity of national and regional identity formation and the confrontations they invoke. More importantly, in many instances, these national and regional identities have turned into identity politics that can take extremist forms, as illustrated by Jewish (not always Israeli) settlers on the West Bank, white supremacists in Western countries, Muslim extremist organizations in various countries with a Muslim majority, and Hindu nationalists in India.

Self-identification as discussed so far focuses on the national and regional levels. But (self)-identification also takes place on a global scale. In the 1950s, during the Cold War, Western countries distinguished between the (rich) 'First World' and (poor) 'Third World', with communist countries occupying the position of 'Second World'. Later, a dichotomy was made between 'Developed' and 'Underdeveloped' countries, which in turn was changed into what was considered the more politically correct terminology of 'Developed' and 'Developing' countries. From the 1990s onwards, with the rise of former 'developing' countries like India, Brazil, South Africa, China and several Southeast Asian countries as economic powers, a new terminology came into place: the global North and the global South. This distinction is made in several ways. One is economic: the countries of the global North are said to be in political and economic decline, whereas those of the global South are, or are expected to be, in a political and economic lift. Another distinction is political and based on a post-colonial resentment: the global South is accusing the global North of not living up to moral, democratic and international legal standards it claims to uphold. In other words, the global South is challenging the global North's assumed position of superiority. An example is Israel's 2023-24 war in Gaza: most countries in the global North maintained their support of Israel, while most countries in the global South supported the Palestinians, and South Africa even brought Israel up on charges of genocide before the International Court of justice.

Putin: sovereignty of 'civilizational states'

According to Russian president Putin, the world is divided in civilizations, and each civilization is ruled by several powerful states. Only such 'civilizational states' are entitled to sovereignty and leadership within their civilizations. The other states in that civilization have no full sovereignty.

(Maria Lagutina et. al., *The Routledge Handbook of Russian International Relations Studies*, 2023)

Individual identification

We now live in times when people increasingly take the initiative to self-identify rather than conform to labels or assumptions imposed by others. This may put them outside of the group that they would normally be identified with, like those considered to be men who self-identify as women. Self-identification and the identification by others may also yield very different perceptions: someone who self-identifies as an aristocrat may be identified by others as a black person, just like the person who self-identifies as the CEO of a company may be identified by others as a woman. Scholars have been trying to come up with labels that can serve as neutral identifiers. That has turned out to be challenging because the charged historical legacy of some terminology.

Race

'Race' is one of these terms: it was used to refer to hereditary qualities of groups of people. This was a common practice all over the world: the Chinese, for instance, considered people with dark skins or 'ash-white' skins to be inferior. However, it was the Europeans who brought this notion to a global level. In the eighteenth and nineteenth centuries, the biological sciences in Europe tried to categorize all living things, including humankind. They did not only identify but also hierarchized the so-called human races. It was the kind of scientific research that quickly had political and social repercussions because it was used to justify the way Europeans (including those living in Australia and the two Americas) perceived the world in which they envisaged themselves the pinnacle of power and civilization. The notion of race thus became very much part of the European colonial practices and terminology that was applied across the world.

> **Origin of 'race'**
> The first use of the term 'race' has been traced back to fifteenth century Spain, where the three religious communities – Christians, Jews, Muslims – were called *razzas*. This term denoted a human quality that was based on blood 'purity' and ancestry. Hence, Muslims and Jews who converted to Catholicism were not considered 'real' Christians, and even their children and grandchildren retained the name *morisco* (for Christians of Muslim origin) and *converso* (for Christians of Jewish origin).

There has been overall academic consensus since the 1950s that the notion of 'race' holds little meaning in the biological and natural sciences and that categories of human 'races' are artificial. Genetic analyses have shown that there is enormous genetic diversity *within* so-called 'races' (like white, black, or other) while only a small percentage of genetic diversity exists *between* these races. In other words, the notion of a biological race based on an isolated gene pool is factually untrue. However, the phenotypes (the visible appearances) of human beings still play an important role in social interactions. Social scientists, when studying how social groups interact, see the need to use the terminology of 'race' when discussing social interactions based on phenotype. Today, the notion of 'race' is therefore a socio-political rather than a scientific concept.

> **'Race does not travel'**
> Racial identification (when people are said to be 'white', or 'black', or 'coloured', or otherwise) differs from social place to place and is therefore context related.
> (Paul C. Taylor, *Race. A Philosophical Introduction*, 2022 (3rd edition))

Racism

The use of racial concepts is not a recent phenomenon. It is of all times and all peoples. But Western racism stands out in a very specific way because it is the legacy of a past in which the Western world had so much influence in the world that they could define race and impose it on the daily lives of most of the world population.

While the notion of race has since then been discarded in most academic disciplines, the notion of racism has become very popular in the Humanities. This may sound paradoxical, but it is not, because there are two different elements at play: *race* is about biological quality, while *racism* is about social behavior. Racism is based on differences in phenotypes and on the assumption that these differences also represent different cultural, intellectual or even biological qualities.

We must also keep in mind that what constitutes racism is often determined by national contexts. Much academic knowledge today about racism is produced by American universities, where the historical context of trans-Atlantic slavery and particular forms of slavery and ensuing forms of discrimination play a central role in these academic discussions. These circumstances are different from, for instance, the issue of race in South America where the Spanish conquerors and colonizers upheld different racial concepts and practices compared to those that affected black people in North America. And the notions of race and racism were yet again different in the experiences and practices in Africa, the Arab world, India, and South-East Asia.

> '**Whiteness**' is a concept that is used in racism discourse to describe social power structures that prevailed among middle and upper classes in Western societies during times of colonialism. Whiteness stands for what is assumed to be the average standard of living that, in turn, is considered by those in power to be the measure stick of all society. Whiteness, therefore, is not necessarily related to skin colour: it is an imagined state of being that is said to be pervasive across the world. The concept proposes that these structures are still dominant in Western societies, but also on a global scale.

Other terms

While the concept of 'racism' has become one of the more prevalent concepts used in Humanities to understand social interactions, other terminology is also still in use. The result is an array of notions with overlapping meanings. For instance, whereas race refers to the phenotype of a person or people, **ethnicity** refers to a common culture and origin. For instance, black people can have different ethnicities (Caribbean, West-African, Afro-American). Another term, already used in this textbook, is **nation**, which refers to a community that has (or perceives) a bond based on culture, language, history, and religion.

This terminology can become quite confusing. For instance, the term **nationality** never refers to membership of a nation, but always to that of state. And not all people belonging to the same nation share the same ethnicity. Imagine, for example, people of Iranian origin who have lived in Germany for three generations and have

German nationality: to what ethnicity and nation do they belong? Often this is a matter of (self-)identification more than biological or social accuracy.

Nation or ethnicity?

Nation and ethnicity are almost synonyms: they both refer to a group of people that share a common culture, background and origin. In common parlance, however, it appears that 'ethnicity' also refers to the phenotype (the visible appearances) of the group members.

A term that used to be popular among social scientists and historians during the 1960s, is **class**. This refers to a social standing based on wealth and, as a derivative of that wealth, a social position that can be hereditary. For instance, aristocrats derived their social status from their wealth, which used to be the income from the lands or commercial enterprises they owned, and their children would benefit from this. Today, even though the aristocracy may have lost much of its standing, having the means to afford good education, health care and housing, contributes to one's social advancement and position in society. Typical of class – and opposed to markers like ethnicity, gender or race – is that social positions can be lost or attained, which usually depends on the person's income. The relation with the other markers is that every racial, ethnic or national group has class stratifications. However, ethnicity often trumps class: people may be very rich but can still be looked down upon if their family pedigree, ethnic background or color of their skin does not match that of the dominant group, for instance.

The complexity of 'diversity'

Companies, governments, universities, and other institutions in Western countries try to overcome the 'white' exclusivity of their staff, employees and students by implementing so-called diversity policies. However, the focus thereby is often on race and ethnicity, and little on class. By overlooking this social-economic dimension, the diversity runs the risk of being lopsided.

One other term of social classification is **gender.** This is a category that is found in all other categories. The trend of individuals determining and proclaiming their own identity is perhaps best demonstrated by the case of gender: the traditional dichotomies of man-woman and homosexual-heterosexual have been opened up to include a wide array of gender identities. While this may appear to be a new development, the novelty of it is not the existence of these multiple identities – these have existed for as long as humankind – but the fact that they have become part of public and political debate.

> **Transgender in Iran**
>
> In Iran, transgender operations are allowed and widely practiced. However, only one of two outcomes is allowed: the person can only be a man or a woman. All other gender modalities are not accepted, nor is homosexuality which is a capital crime.

Scholars realize that all these categories can be fluid and overlapping and can come together in one and the same person. For this reason, the notion of **intersectionality** was introduced. This concept holds that a person's vulnerability to discrimination or oppression is often not caused by a single category of identity. An example is the black woman, where race and gender play 'intersecting' roles in the manner how she is treated. The status of class will play an additional role: is this black woman well-to-do and with a high-profile job, or does she live in a poor neighborhood doing night shifts?

> **Gender statistics**
>
> "Between 2019 and 2022, nearly 40% of countries – home to over 1.1. billion women and girls in 2022 – stagnated or declined on gender equality."
> (*2024 SDG Gender Index*)
>
> Best performing countries (2024) in closing the gender gap in economy, health, education, politics:
> 1. Iceland
> 2. Finland
> 3. Norway
> 4. New Zealand
> 5. Sweden
> 6. Nicaragua
> 7. Germany
> 8. Namibia
> 9. Ireland
> 10. Spain
> (*Global Gender Gap Report*, 2024)

Globalization and glocalization of identity

We have seen that identity plays a role on the individual level and increasingly also on the national level (identity politics), sometimes even on a global level (North-South tensions). But two events that happened locally were to propel the issues of race and gender to a global level. In 2018, the accusations of sexual abuse against Hollywood tycoon Harvey Weinstein contributed to the worldwide popularity of the social movement known as #MeToo. It would reopen debates across the globe on power and violence in gender relations. A year later, in 2019, the killing of a black man by the name of George Floyd by a white police officer did the same for the social movement known as Black Lives Matter: their protests in the United States sparked mass demonstrations across the world.

In both instances, the focus was on power and violence in race and gender relations. These issues had been raised time and again for decades but now gained a global attention that seems to have brought on a significant change: not only did victims feel empowered to speak out and did perpetrators have less of an opportunity to get away with their behavior, but progress was also made on a governmental and institutional level to address these social structures. At the same time, however, there were strong counter forces across the globe that wanted to maintain the dominant structures of the man-woman gender division, preferably embedded in a patriarchal system. In Western societies, a racial component was added to these counter forces that argued for preserving the nation's authenticity.

Further reading

Samir Amin, "The Future of Global Polarization," *Africa Today*, Vol. 40, No. 4, 1993, pp. 75-86

Thomas Carothers and Andrew O'Dondhue (eds.), *Democracies Divided: The Global Challenge of Political Polarization*, Brookings Institution Press, 2019

Francis Fukuyama, *Identity: The demand for dignity and the politics of resentment*, Farrar, Straus and Giroux, 2018

Joseph L. Graves Jr. and Alan H. Goodman, *Racism, not Race. Answers to frequently asked questions*, Columbia University, 2021

Amy Gutman (ed.), *Multiculturalism: Examining the Politics of Recognition*, Princeton University Press, 1994

Paul C. Taylor, *Race. A Philosophical Introduction*, Polity Pr, 2022 (3rd edition)

Peter Wade, *Race. an Introduction*, Cambridge University Press, 2015

CHAPTER 3

Equality and self-determination

The notion of equality is not new to humankind: several religions claim it as a cornerstone of their creed (because everyone is a believer regardless of rank or status) and it was declared a key element to the 'rights of men' as included in the French and American constitutions in the late 18th century. However, when in 1776 the American Declaration of Independence declared that "all men are created equal," this was not referring to women or those who were enslaved. And in Europe of the nineteenth and early twentieth century, only rich (white) men had the right to vote. Communist Russia and China implemented a strict equality, but ultimately these states were run by a small elite.

It took until the 1950s to make a serious start with putting the value of equality into practice. True equality – that is: regardless of gender, color, social class or religion – became enshrined in the constitutions of most states. Often it remained a mere intention and the goal of true equality has in many instances still not been reached, mostly because of obstruction by embedded social structures like patriarchy and racism. But given its legal status, equality was something that could be claimed by those who were willing to fight for it. Equality had become the rule, even if social reality did not live up to it. This was a distinct difference from the many centuries preceding the twentieth, when the opposite was the case: inequality was the rule, and only sometimes did social reality live up to it.

> **Patriarchy** is the main obstacle to gender equality. Patriarchy is defined as "a system of relationships, beliefs, and values embedded in political, social, and economic systems that structure gender inequality between men and women" (Catherine Nash in *International Encyclopedia of Human Geography*, 2020). Patriarchy has a very long tradition in human history and can therefore be considered a **global structure**.

Tolerance

In the past centuries, the closest one could get to equality was tolerance. Today one still hears the call for tolerance, often in conjunction with equality. But tolerance is a different concept entirely. Tolerance means that one endures something that one disagrees with. In earlier times, societies were called tolerant when people with different ideas or behavior were nevertheless accepted. Usually this was the case with religion. Such tolerance was exercised by those in power: they made the decision to be benevolent towards those with views or beliefs with which they disagreed or simply disliked. They could just as easily have decided not to do so.

Toleration (i.e., the practice of tolerance), therefore, is always connected to power and to a situation of inequality: those in power may dislike a belief, or a behavior, or a certain race of people, but nevertheless decide to exercise tolerance. A Catholic King may tolerate his Jewish subjects, a general may tolerate insubordination, a mother may tolerate her children being impolite. One never speaks of toleration in the opposite direction: Jewish subjects do not 'tolerate' their Catholic King, soldiers will not 'tolerate' their general, and children will not 'tolerate' their mother. The reasons to tolerate something or not can range from pragmatism (toleration to avoid conflict) to morality (toleration as a moral obligation to allow for another person's convictions).

This is what we may call **power tolerance**, and this has been the practice all over the world throughout the centuries. This changed radically, however, with the introduction of equality as a political and social right. Because if all people are equal, regardless of gender, color, social class, or religion, and everyone is equally entitled to the same rights and freedoms, who, then, decides to tolerate people or not? Not the king, not the government, not the majority. Equality therefore became one of the most drastic changes in the social fabric of societies worldwide. It would gradually uproot long-lived social structures and traditions that were based on distinctions among people.

In doing so, the notion of tolerance would gain an additional meaning. In a society based on equality, toleration has come to mean that one needs to tolerate the differences one is being confronted with. Equality dictates that all people, regardless of their differences, have the right to be who they want to be. Toleration has therefore shifted from power toleration to **acceptance toleration**. This does not mean that power toleration has disappeared – to the contrary, in many societies one observes that the claim for equal treatment ('I claim the right to be who I want to be, just like anyone else has that same claim') is often countered by power tolerance ('your exclusive behavior is not tolerated, you should adapt to the majority').

Equality is a global trend that shows all the signs of becoming a global structure, because for most people today the notion of equality is self-evident. But to establish equality as a legal right does not mean that it is socially accepted. One may even wonder if there are places today where equality has been fully and truly established. But it remains a fact that the notion of equality has firmly established itself in the minds of people today. From a historical perspective, this is a revolutionary development, and we are still in the middle of it.

Equality, equity, and equivalence

Equality among people

The principle of equality is one of the key notions used in constitutions and international human rights agreements. Equality was first interpreted as a legal right to equal treatment in similar cases (see chapter 'Human Rights'). For instance, men, women, people of color, or disabled people should all have equal access to jobs (provided they meet the qualifications for that job), and equal pay for the same job. The means to reach this type of equality was the creation of **equal opportunity** for everyone: everyone had the right to vote, to apply for a job, to participate in meetings and races, to receive the same salary.

But even when the principle of equality was translated into law, practice showed differently. The *rule* of equality showed to be insufficient to reach the *goal* of equality: in most societies where the rule of equality was upheld, differences in gender, ethnicity, social class remained intact. Apparently, mechanisms of discrimination among people were – and are – still in place as patterns of pervasive social practices and structures that are hard to combat. For instance, a building may be 'open for all' but it isn't if it only has staircases; a race does not provide the same opportunity for winning if one person is well nourished and the other is underfed; and in a school program that treats all pupils equally, pupils with educated parents who can help with schoolwork have greater advantage than those who do not.

> **'Empty idea of equality'**
>
> Equality has no value content of its own. Consequently, giving everyone an income of 100 euro serves equality as much as giving everyone nothing. This is called the 'empty idea of equality'.
>
> (Peter Westen, *The Empty Idea of Equality*, 1982)

To remedy this, the notion of **equity** was introduced. Whereas equality stands for treating everyone the same by providing equal opportunity for all, equity allows for treating each individual differently depending on needs and backgrounds, and by doing so levelling the playing field for all participants. Equity, therefore, argues for tailor-made approaches for people so that they have the opportunity reach the position in which they can participate and compete equally with others. Someone had voiced this idea as follows: "Equality is giving everyone a shoe, equity is giving everyone a shoe that fits."[*]

It must be noted that equity, too, has its critics, the predominant argument being that equity's individual differentiation may lead to preferential treatment, which is considered contrary to equality. Should, for instance, preference been given to hiring women, people of color, disabled people, or others? It is against equal treatment, but the supporters of equity will argue that one first needs to create a balanced composition of personnel before one can start treating them equally. From this perspective, equity is the way to arrive at an equal situation. An interesting element of the concept of equity is that it has been given much importance in the international discussions on sustainable development (see chapter 'Sustainable Development').

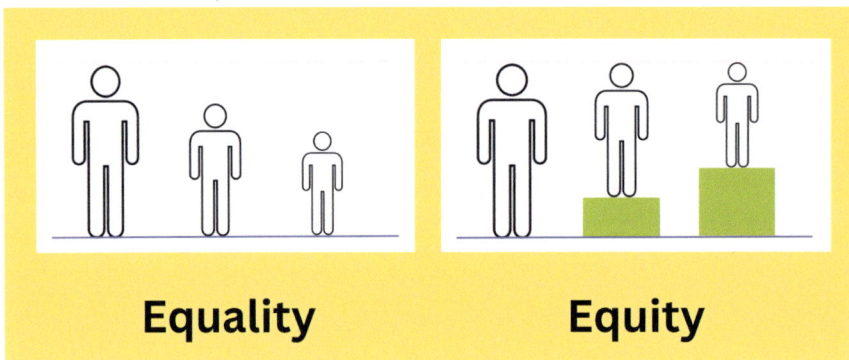

Figure III.3.1 Equality and equity

Another response by the critics of the notion of equality is that of **equivalence**. This plays out mostly in the situation of gender relations between men and women. The advocates of equivalence argue that men and women are biologically different and are therefore not to be treated as the same. But rather than arguing for a patriarchal order between men and women, they call for 'equality in dignity': men and women are said to be different people with different potentials (and some say: different roles), but they are equal in those different positions. This 'different but equal' has been heavily criticized by supporters of the (legal) notion of equality who point at the risk that 'equality in dignity' allows for denying women the same rights as men.

---

[*]   Attributed to Susan K. Gardner, Oregon State University.

Equality among states

Equality not only pertains to people. A similar development is taking place among states. The traditional hierarchy of states – the rich and militarily powerful at the top – has been disrupted by the establishment of the United Nations and by the de-colonization process: the number of states has since then quadrupled and every state is officially an equal among peers. Perhaps China, America, or Russia consider themselves rulers of the world, but every other state of that world is accorded the same equal standing as they have. And former colonizers might still look down upon countries that once were their colonies but these now need to be treated as equal counterparts.

In the same way as equality, the notion of equity also plays a role in international relations, even if the term 'equity' is not used in this respect. In the debates on climate change, for example, many countries of the global North argue that efforts need to be made by all countries equally. But many countries of the global South, while agreeing with the need for action on climate change, argue that they are already disadvantaged and therefore should not be burdened on an equal footing with rich and developed countries. This is, in effect, a claim to equitable treatment.

Even though equality among states is the rule of international law, it tells us nothing about the true power dynamics that are at play in the world. Luxembourg is a tiny country in the European Union, where France and Germany call the shots. The same is the case for Nigeria and South Africa in the African Union, and Russia, China, and America on the world stage. The political reality shows a continuous powerplay based on strength. Nevertheless, the generally accepted yardstick is the equality of states and of persons. But even so, the problem is the implementation of equality: there are no international legal mechanisms to uphold equal treatment between states, even when it is required by international law. Unequal treatment in the form of differentiation, favoritism and even discrimination is therefore still part of international politics.

Self-determination

Equality offers the opportunity to be who you want to be: there is no need to conform oneself to others, as everyone has the same right to live how they want to. A similar situation also applies to states, but here it is called self-determination. Self-determination is the right of a nation to determine its own destiny. Self-determination can take different forms: as a state, or as a form of minority rights within a state.

Self-determination is a relatively recent concept. It was closely linked to the ideology of nationalism in the nineteenth century, because both self-determination and nationalism claim a territorial space in which a nation can live according to its own customs and desires. And just like nationalism, the notion of self-determination became a slogan that mobilized people, first by Lenin who called for the self-determination of the proletariat, but perhaps even more so by the American president Woodrow Wilson in 1918 at the peace talks after the First World War. The German, Austro-Hungarian and Ottoman Empires had been defeated, and the victors were deciding what to do with the vast territories of these conquered empires and with the many different nations that lived in these territories. Wilson then famously declared: "National aspirations must be respected; people may now be dominated and governed only by their own consent. 'Self-determination' is not a mere phrase; it is an imperative principle of action."[*]

For some nations, like the Poles and the Hungarians and Czechs, this resulted in creation of their own states. Others, like the Kurds and the Middle Eastern Arabs, were disappointed that they were not granted statehood. It also quickly became clear that self-determination was not intended for the many peoples living under colonial rule. But the idea would resonate strongly around the world. Later, in 1945, the United Nations adopted self-determination as one of its goals, placing it notably alongside equality: "To develop friendly relations among nations based on respect for the principle of equal rights and self-determination of peoples."[**] This would become one of the key motivations and justifications for people to claim independence or autonomy within a state.

Examples of minority nations that have autonomy within a state

Native Americans in the United States (also: North American Indians, Indian Tribes, or Indigenous people of America) have limited rule over their own lands where they can apply their own laws and have their own law enforcement. However, they are subject to Federal law.

Kurds in Iraq have an autonomous region in north Iraq with their own government, parliament, and judiciary system, and that pursues its own foreign policy. However, it is part of the federal administration of Iraq.

Catalans in Spain are one of the 17 'autonomous communities' (*comunidad autónoma*) that has limited political and administrative powers. Their call for full independence in 2017 was not recognized by the state of Spain.

'Bantustans' were supposed to be independent, self-governing territories for black people in South Africa during apartheid, but in practice they remained controlled by the government of South Africa.

---

[*]   Woodrow Wilson, adress to Congress on International Order, 11 February 1918.
[**]   Article 1 (2) of the United Nations Charter.

Like equality, self-determination is a recent global trend that appears to be developing into a global structure. Self-determination may be enshrined as a fundamental right, but this does not guarantee that it will always be respected as there are enough examples in the world of peoples ('nations') being denied their right to self-determination. In many cases this denial is justified on the grounds that it would undermine the sovereignty of the state to which such nations belong.

Palestine in the United Nations

Several Israeli government leaders in the period between 1948 and 1993 have argued that Palestinians were not a nation by themselves but part of the larger 'Arab' nation. This argument was used to deny Palestinians the right of self-determination and, consequently, their right to their own state. In 1993 Israel did recognize the Palestinians as a nation, but not as a state. In 2012, the 'state of Palestine' was given observer status in the United Nations. By 2024, Palestine was recognized as a state by 143 of the 193 states in the world but was still denied (by American veto) full membership as a state in the United Nations. This left the nation of Palestinians with the paradoxical situation that they could not fully exercise their right of self-determination and establish a functioning state, but at the same time were recognized as such by most of the world.

Further reading

Thomas Christiano, "Self Determination and the Human Right to Democracy" in: Rowan Cruft (ed.), *Philosophical Foundations of Human Rights*, Oxford University Press, 2015, pp. 459–480

Darrin M. MacMahon, *Equality. The History of an Elusive Idea*, Basic Books, 2023

Amartya Sen, *Inequality Reexamined*, Harvard University Press, 1995

Steven Smith, *Equality and diversity. Value incommensurability and the politics of recognition*, Policy Press, 2011

Tom Sparks, *Self-Determination in the International Legal System. Whose Claim, to What Right?*, Bloomsbury 2023

CHAPTER 4

Secularization and religionization

The twentieth century has witnessed an interesting turn in the global structure of religion: in the first half of the twentieth century, until the 1970s, the world was averse to religion, while since the 1970s the world has witnessed the increasing importance of religion in all facets of life, including social and political.

Secularization

From the late nineteenth century, the world witnessed a gradual decline of religion in two ways: it lost its importance to people and its institutional importance to the state. In other words, people were less religious than before, and religious institutions did not have the same power as before. This process is called secularization.

The exact reasons for secularization are still debated, but it is generally believed that it was motivated by modernity and the popularity of rationalism. **Rationalism** had its roots primarily in 18th century European thought where knowledge, gained through facts and empirical inquiry became prevalent and a source of refutation of beliefs held by religion. This way of thinking was spread around the world, mainly through colonial educational institutions, and it challenged the self-evidence of truths upheld by religious beliefs. **Modernity** also originated in the Western world and has multiple meanings, but is used here in terms of advances in technology (steam engines, electricity, telephone and telegraph, etc.) and state institutionalization (bureaucracy, codification, postal service, parliament, etc.). Modernity gave people self-confidence and a sense of progress away from the mostly religious traditions and institutions that were now considered redundant. Modernity, also, spread around the world through colonialism, but it was particularly prevalent in decolonizing countries: most leaders of new post-colonial states preferred a modern state similar in structure to that of their former colonizing masters.

This combined development of secularization, modernity and rationalism was coined by scholars as the **secularization thesis**, which, in summary, argued that the more modernity advanced, the more religion would disappear. And indeed, all over the world, including Asia, Africa, South America, one could observe the secularization of societies, especially in the period between the 1950s and the 1970s. In retrospect, is it difficult to imagine that female students in the universities of Kabul, Tehran, or Baghdad wore short skirts and no headscarves (see image). Similarly, religious institutions like the Catholic Church, or the Hindu or Muslim clergy, had little if any influence on society and state affairs.

Figure III.4.1 Students in Kabul, Afghanistan, 1972

Two religious homelands

Examples of this secularization are the countries of Israel and Pakistan. Both were created as religious homelands: Pakistan in 1947 as homeland for the Muslims in British India, and Israel in 1948 as homeland for the Jews from Europe. Their stories of conception, birth, and growth are quite similar. In the late nineteenth and early twentieth centuries, Jews in Europe and Muslims in British India, began to think of a place for themselves. While they identified as Jews and Muslims, they did not necessarily mean it in a religious sense. Most European Jews who supported the idea of a Jewish homeland were quite secular, and the same was true of many of the Muslims in British India who entertained a similar idea of a homeland. For both communities, the urge for a homeland was not primarily religious, but was a response to discrimination: the Jews in an increasingly antisemitic Europe, and the Muslims in the Hindu-majority India. Their self-identification as Muslims and Jews was therefore more cultural than purely religious. So, when these homelands finally came into being, they were duly named the Jewish state and the Islamic state, but both states were quite non-religious in their identity and secular in their composition.

This changed in the 1970s. In both countries, the issue of religion increasingly played a role in questions of national identity. Only Jews could obtain Israeli nationality, but who is a Jew? The state of Israel was discussed more in biblical terms, and the claim to the West Bank was justified as a religious birthright. The term anti-Semitism, commonly used to refer to discrimination or hatred of Jews, was now also interpreted to include criticism of Israel. Similarly in Pakistan, questions were raised about non-Muslims serving as ministers in the government, and there were increasing calls for more Islamic legislation. This development is called 'religionization'.

'Religionization'

Since the 1970s, religion has gained in importance everywhere in the world (except in Europe, which has remained secularized for reasons that are still unclear). In this textbook we will call this development '**religionization**', which means that religion became important to people in their personal, societal, and sometimes political lives. Why this happened, and why at this particular time, remains a question and is hotly debated by scholars but there is a consensus that the secularization thesis turned out to be incorrect.

The 'religionization' of the world has manifested itself in different ways. For some, it is a personal matter practiced in the privacy of the home, but many also feel the need to practice this religion together. This has led to places of worship filling up but also to new ones being built. In some cases, these religious gatherings have reached enormous proportions, with huge mosques and mega-churches in Asia or West Africa or the use of stadiums.

For many believers, religion also has a social significance. As a result, the number of religious associations, organizations and societies around the world has grown exponentially. Some would focus on poverty, others on development, health care or emergency relief. Most of them are non-governmental organizations (NGOs), also known as faith-based organizations (FBOs). As such, they are a manifestation of civil society.

But there are also believers for whom religion is a source of inspiration for how society should be governed or structured. Here we enter the realm of politics. For some, this goal is to be achieved through a political party that is founded on religious principles. Others may form lobbying groups to pressure governments to intervene in certain social issues, like abortion in America, or to expand territory, like the occupied lands in Israel, or to enforce religious rules like in India, Pakistan or northern Nigeria. Still others may go as far as to replace the government with some kind of theocracy, as was successfully done in Iran (in 1979) and is being sought by various Muslim groups around the globe.

Religionization means that religion has become important to people in their personal, societal, and sometimes also political lives.

The return of religion

Most scholars agree that religion has grown in importance, but find this difficult to prove. Sociological surveys provide statistics that tell us that by 2050 the number of Muslims will almost equal the number of Christians in the world, and that 4 out of every 10 Christians in the world will live in sub-Saharan Africa (see figure). In these predictions, India will in 2050 retain a Hindu majority but will also have the largest Muslim population of any country in the world, surpassing Indonesia.

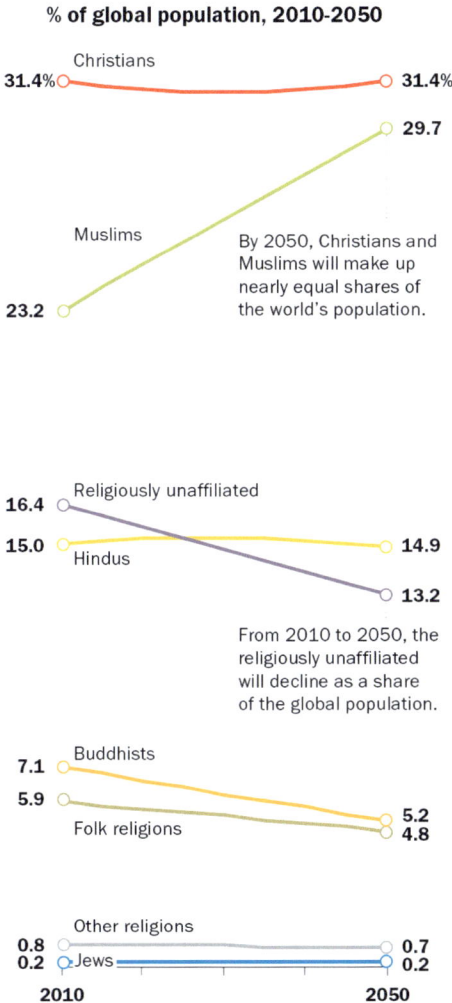

% of global population, 2010-2050

Christians
31.4% ○———————————————○ 31.4%

○ 29.7

Muslims

By 2050, Christians and
Muslims will make up
nearly equal shares of
23.2 ○ the world's population.

Religiously unaffiliated
16.4 ○

15.0 ○
Hindus ○ 14.9

○ 13.2

From 2010 to 2050, the
religiously unaffiliated
will decline as a share
of the global population.

Buddhists
7.1 ○

5.9 ○
○ 5.2
Folk religions ○ 4.8

Other religions
0.8 ○———————————————○ 0.7
0.2 ○ Jews ═══════════════○ 0.2

2010   **2050**

"The Future of World Religions: Population Growth Projections,
2010-2050"

PEW RESEARCH CENTER

Figure III.4.2 Global growth of religion

However, such numbers must be treated with caution because they are demographic statistics that are extrapolations based on expected birth rates. So, if the Christians in a certain country are estimated to be a certain percentage of the population, and their birth rates are predicted to be another percentage, then a calculation is made about the increase or decrease of that Christian population. But such numbers tell us nothing about the religiosity of these people. One can call someone a Hindu or a Muslim or a Christian, but what does religion mean to them, personally, or in their social or political life? Also, there are many people who identify with a religion, but do not even practice it.

More enlightening, therefore, are surveys that examine how people self-identify as regards religion (see figure III.4.3). Such surveys tell us that the countries where people feel most religious are in Africa and Asia (with China as an unknown factor due to lack of research data), and with South America on the rise. It then may be surprising, then, that a country like Iran is not high on the list. This can be explained by the consideration that a state may profile itself as religious and impose religious rules on its population, but this does not necessarily have to reflect how that population feels about religion.

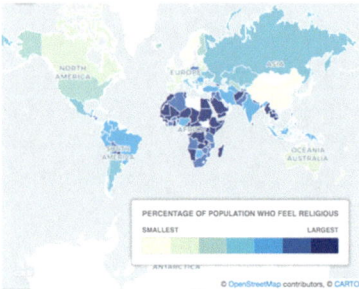

PERCENTAGE OF POPULATION WHO FEEL RELIGIOUS

SMALLEST   LARGEST

© OpenStreetMap contributors, © CARTO

Figure III.4.3 Global experience of religiosity

Has religion, then, returned or, in other words, has it regained its original status and impact? The answer appears to be negative: religion has returned, but in a different form. Religion is not so much a force of power in the hands of the clergy, as it used to be, but in the hands of laypeople, people who are not clergy but who feel knowledgeable and confident enough to speak in name of religion. We may call this the **democratization of religion**: believers do not feel the need to follow religious doctrine or institutions because they prefer to speak and think for themselves. As a result, one observes the popularity of non-institutionalized preachers, sects and organizations. Whereas religion used to have a top-down structure, it has now become a bottom-up force. This means that the domain of religion is not dominated by clergy as it used to be, but by politicians, activists and self-appointed preachers. They do not speak in the name of religious institutions, but in the name of religion itself. And they do not only discuss religion in the private and religious sphere, but also in the material, social and political sphere of today's world. That is why we find religion in today's discourses on topics as disparate as human rights, women's rights, environment, climate change, food production, sustainable development, peace and conflict.

Religious literacy

Secularization is still dominant in Europe. As a result, people have little affinity with and knowledge about religion. This has negatively affected Europeans working in functions abroad, like journalists, diplomats, aid workers: they interact with societies where religion plays a significant role in most domains of everyday social and political life, but they are unable to 'see' it. This is considered an impediment to successful functioning abroad. To remedy that, there are calls to increase their "religious literacy". That does not mean that they must become religious, or that they must like religion, but that they must understand the workings of religion in the modern world.

Further reading

Peter L. Berger (ed.), *The Desecularization of the World: Resurgent Religion and World Politics*, Wm. B. Eerdmans Publishing, 1999

Jacques Berlinerblau, *Secularism: The Basics*, Routledge 2024

Barry A. Kosmin and Ariela Keysar (eds.), *Secularism & Secularity: Contemporary International Perspectives*, Institute for the Study of Secularism in Society and Culture, 2007

Charles Taylor, *A Secular Age*, Harvard University Press, 2007

Scott M. Thomas, *The Global Resurgence of Religion and the Transformations of International Relations*, Palgrave Macmillan, 2005

CHAPTER 5

Transnationalism

Migration is one of the global structures, as we have seen in chapter 'Migration', and so are the resulting **diasporas**, peoples who have permanently settled outside of their place of origin but still retain a bond as a nation. Examples of century-old diasporas are the Jews, Greeks and Chinese, who kept cultural, linguistic, religious and business ties with their community members across the borders.

From the late nineteenth century onward, migration that resulted in permanent settlement abroad increased significantly: Koreans migrated to Russia and China, Chinese and Europeans to the United States, Syrians and Lebanese to South America, Indians to Africa, to name just a few. A new surge of migration also took place after the Second World War, but this time the world witnessed a global inversion of migration: most migration was now towards Europe, at first from former colonies and for the recruitment of laborers from abroad, and later also for political and economic reasons.

Many of these peoples integrated into their new societies by identifying themselves as part of their new home, and many also maintained strong ties with their nation of origin. The interactions that the members of such communities maintain across borders is called **transnationalism.** These interactions usually relate to matters of family, religion or business, and are maintained with the country of origin, but often also with community members in other countries. In such instances, the identity of these people is also called a transnational identity because it transgresses national borders.

A **diaspora** consists of members belonging to a nation that have permanently settled in different places outside their place of origin and who retain a bond based on shared culture, language, religion. When this bond translates into cross-border interactions among people of this nation – like business or family relations – this is referred to as **transnationalism**.

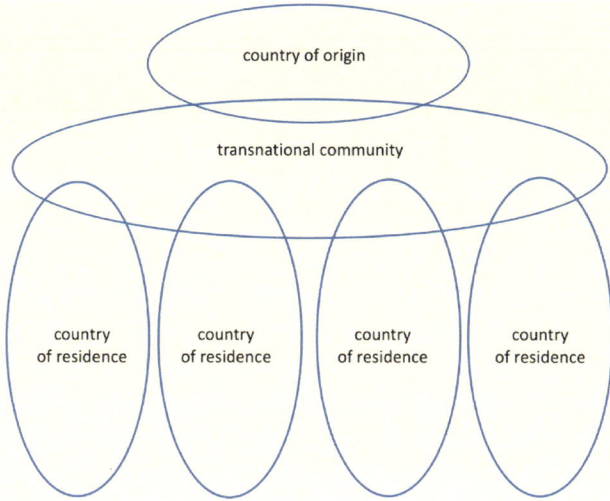

Figure III.5.1 Transnationalism

Transnational perspectives

Transnationalism as such is not new, but its occurrence has increased significantly since the 1990s. The reasons for this augmentation are not entirely clear but might be attributed to the increase of national self-identification (see chapter 'Identity') and to the increased availability of means of transport and communication. Irrespective of the exact reasons, academics and policy makers have started to pay more attention to this phenomenon. It has also provided new perspectives on a number of issues that were otherwise overlooked or considered self-evident. These issues will be discussed below.

National identity

There is a general assumption that growing up in a nation-state shapes people's thinking, identity and outlook on the world and, in effect, contributes to the identification with the 'nation' through its shared history, culture and language. But this assumption is challenged by the citizens of that state who have migrated from other parts of the world. Will they give up their own history, culture and language? Or merge it with that of their new home country? And, more importantly, will these processes take place within the confines of the nation-state? Transnationalism shows that this is not the case. From the perspective of transnationalism, therefore, the notion of the nation-state as a closed container in which a national identity is being shaped, needs to be revisited.

Belonging

Belonging is a complex notion, that may be described as the emotion of 'feeling at home' which, in turn, is based on the bond that one feels with one's social, political and cultural environment, and is closely related to the concept of **imagined community**. However, this particular nation-state perspective may conflict with the transnational perspective. Do members of transnational communities feel a sense of belonging to their community, or to their country of residence, or to their country of origin, or perhaps to all of these simultaneously? For instance, the culture of the new country of residence may give a certain meaning to family or work relations, while the culture of the country of origin may add another layer of meaning to these relations. In that case, the culture of the country of origin is not being left behind but is taken along to the new country of residence. In other words, members of transnational communities share several social spheres or, as sociologists have termed it, **'habitats of meaning'** or environments that contain their own sets of values and meaning. Managing the multiple habitats of meaning is not always easy and may lead to what is referred to as **liminality**, which refers to a feeling of being 'in-between'. This term was originally used to describe the transition in rites of passage in non-industrial and traditional communities but is now also used to explain political and cultural transitions in general.

> **Liminality** is the feeling of not really belonging, being 'here nor there'. It describes a temporary state of people who are in transition. It can apply to a variety of human situations, like migration, religious conversion, gender identity.

Loyalty

Whereas belonging has a socio-cultural meaning, the related notion of loyalty has a socio-political connotation. It can be defined as the unconditional fidelity that one has towards one's family, community, leader, religion or country. The quality of the unconditional is important: people loyal to a leader, for instance, tend to be forgiving for the leader's faults and the same is true for family members, religions and states. Loyalty also works the other way round: families, communities, leaders, religions or countries expect loyalty from its members.

But do members of transnational communities feel loyalty towards their community, their country of residence or their country of origin, or perhaps to all of these at the same time? These questions are not only important from a social perspective, they have strong political implications as well. Nationals of a country may feel sorry for someone who lacks a sense of belonging to that society, but they may be suspicious or even hostile to someone who lacks loyalty towards their country. Even though loyalty can be hard to measure, it manifests itself in very diverse ways. For instance, people may frown on transnational citizens cheering for the national team of their country of origin rather than for that of their country of residence. Or transnationals may oppose military involvement of their country of residence in another country because their geopolitical views are rooted in the perspective of their country of origin rather than their country of residence. While this doesn't necessarily mean that these transnationals are less loyal to their country of residence, their loyalty may be questioned by others.

Foreign influences

Another aspect of transnationalism is the influence exerted by countries of origin on people who have migrated abroad and have become residents there. The reasons for this can vary. They can be economic when a country of origin is dependent on a steady inflow of remittances. Cultural or religious support for fellow nationals can be another reason, with countries of origin like Japan and Mexico who provide language schools abroad, or Turkey and Morocco who send imams.

Some countries of origin reach out because they still consider these transnationals to be 'their' nationals. This can have a legal dimension when a migrant retains the nationality of the country of origin, which usually extends also to the next generations. Sometimes this involvement may have a political dimension, for instance when migrants still have voting rights in their country of origin where politicians might want these votes. This happened during the Turkish elections in 2019, when President Erdogan campaigned in Europe to secure the vote of people of Turkish origin who, due to their Turkish nationality, still retained the right to vote in Turkey.

Not all migrants who settled in their new country are pleased with this kind of attention from their countries of origin, especially not when they are the second or third generation and no longer have much of a connection with their country of origin. The new home country of these migrants may also feel uneasy or even threatened by the scrutiny its nationals receive from their country of origin.

Double nationality

Certain states hold that their nationals retain the nationality of the state, even if they have become the nationals of other countries. The nationality law of such state of origin often dictates that the nationality is passed on to the children, so that the next generations of migrants retain the nationality from their country of origin. In such cases, the men can remain eligible for military service in the country of origin. People with such nationality can usually do little about it: it is not the person but the state that can retract a nationality. So while the new home country may prohibit double nationality (that is: nationality of the new country as well as the country of origin), this prohibition cannot be enforced in these instances unless the country of origin retracts the nationality, which is very rare.

Further reading

Zain Abdullah, "Transnationalism and the Politics of Belonging: African Muslim Circuits in Western Spaces", *Journal of Muslim Minority Affairs*, Vol. 32, No. 4, pp. 427-449

Caroline B. Brettell, "Global Spaces/Local Places: Transnationalism, Diaspora, and the Meaning of Home", *Identities: Global Studies in Culture and Power*, Vol.13, No.3, 2006, pp. 327-334

Robin Cohen, *Global Diasporas. An Introduction*, Routledge, 2023

Thomas Faist, Margit Fauser and Eveline Reisenauer, *Transnational Migration*, Polity Press, 2013

Steffen Mau, *Social Transnationalism: Lifeworlds Beyond the Nation-State*, Routledge, 2010

Steven Vertovec, *Transnationalism*, Routledge, 2009

CHAPTER 6

Democracy and good governance

Up until the 1940s, it was still a matter of debate what constitutes the best form of government: communism, fascism, democracy or some type of autocratic rule. This debate was literally fought out in Europe but was also very pertinent in the colonized lands across the world for whom independence was impending. After 1945, a lot of states opted for a democratic state model, but its opposite – some type of autocratic rule – was also very popular around the world, especially from the 1960s onward. One of the reasons for the wide spread of autocratic regimes is that the great powers of the time – the United States and the Soviet-Union – allowed it, preferring a controllable dictator over an unpredictable democracy. In the famous words of an American president about a South American dictator: "He may be a son of a bitch, but he is our son of a bitch."* As long as rulers made a clear choice for one side or the other in the Cold War, they could get away with almost anything.

The popularity of democracy

This changed in the 1990s with the implosion of the Soviet Union and the subsequent end of the Cold War. From that moment onwards, democracy was promoted worldwide as the best form of government. To some this was for reasons of idealism, to others the reasons were more pragmatic ('democracies don't wage war' was an often used maxim), and yet others thought democracies would be the best way to promote international cooperation and prosperity.

Why democracy?

"Democracies, after all, are more likely to be stable, less likely to wage war. They strengthen civil society. They can provide people with the economic and political opportunities to build their futures in their own homes, not to flee their borders. Our efforts to help build more democracies will make us all more secure, more prosperous, and more successful as we try to make this era of terrific change our friend and not our enemy."

(President Bill Clinton's address to the UN General Assembly, 1994)

The popularity of democracy from the 1990s onwards was shown by the widespread demonstrations of that time calling for democracy. Let's make a quick tour to get a

---

* Franklin D. Roosevelt about Nicaraguan president Somoza, in 1939.

feel for the unprecedented extend of these demonstrations. It started in 1989 with revolts in several countries that until then had been satellite states of the Soviet Union: Poland, the Baltic states Latvia, Estonia and Lithuania, Hungary, East Germany, Bulgaria, Czechoslovakia and Romania. In all these countries the mass demonstrations and civil resistance led to a non-violent overthrow of the regimes (except for Romania where the Romanian dictator, Ceausescu and his wife were tried and executed on live television). In the same year of 1989, on the other side of the world, similar demonstrations were taking place in Mongolia and China. Elsewhere in the world, in the years of 1989 and 1990, several African and Central and South American countries also made the shift to a more democratic state system.

These changes of governance did not always go smoothly, but they did create a world-wide sense of optimism and consequently were a source of concern for dictators still in power. After a decade of silence, a new round of mass demonstrations against dictatorial regimes became world news, this time with poetic names: the Rose revolution in Georgia in 2003, the Orange revolution in the Ukraine in 2004, and the Tulip revolution in Kirgizia in 2005. All these revolts led to a non-violent overthrow of the sitting regimes. And after the 2009 mass demonstrations in Iran in support of a liberal candidate for the presidency, a series of uprisings happened in 2011 that became known as the Arab Spring, toppling the long sitting regimes of Tunisia, Libya, Egypt and Yemen. (Similar demonstrations in Bahrein and Syria were oppressed.)

There was again a lull until 2019, when the world witnessed a new series of non-violent mass demonstrations, mostly driven by young people, and this time all over the world: the most famous and lengthy one was in Hong Kong, but protracted mass demonstrations also took place in Algeria, Iran, Lebanon, Iraq, Morocco and Sudan in the Middle East, Bolivia and Chile in South America, and Catalonia in Europe.

Revolt or revolution?

Many of the mass demonstration since the 1990s were referred to as 'revolution.' However, in most cases the aim of these demonstrations and uprisings was to topple the regime, not to replace the entire political system. The apt term would then be 'revolt', that is a popular uprising against those in power. Complete overturns of political systems ('revolutions') are rare, the main examples being the revolutions in America (1775), France (1789), Russia (1917), China (1949), Iran (1979).

The globalization of mass protests

All these protests were national, that is: they took place within a single country and mostly called for fairer and more democratic governance. But thanks to the advanced possibilities of social media, the protesters of the 2010s were keenly aware of each other. They were not only watching each other, they were also learning from each other, inspiring each other, using each other's techniques, as well as slogans and symbols. The Spanish slogan *No Paseran* ('They shall not pass!') was not only spraypainted on the walls in Catalonia and Chile, but also in Hong Kong and Iraq. The defiant gesture of raising one's hands to indicate peaceful intent when facing the police during demonstrations was copied from the Black Lives Matter protests in America. And the conscientious act of cleaning up after the demonstrations could be observed from Hong Kong to Lebanon.

Regardless of these global connections and inspirations, the protests mentioned so far had distinctly national aims. This was different for other types of protest movements that were global in both their aims and character. It is perhaps not surprising that the most prominent of them emerged in the same period of 2018 and 2019: #MeToo, Black Lives Matter, Extinction Rebellion, and Fridays for Future. These protests took place on social media as much as they did on the streets and were of a regional and global rather than national level. The reason for the global scope is that these movements addressed issues that are relevant for people all over the world: climate change, power and violence based on gender and race.

The building blocks of democracy

It's one thing to demonstrate for democracy, it's quite another to know what democracy entails. This is not the place to elaborate the political history and philosophy of democracy, but a brief explanation of recent developments is needed to understand the global complexities of today. Four elements jump out: sovereignty of the people, elections, civil society and good governance.

Sovereignty of the people

Most demonstrations against governments today are not meant to turn political systems into democracies (because most of these countries are formally already democracies) but protest the ways in which these political systems have become corrupted and abused. The demonstrators claim a democratic right, namely that they are entitled to have a say in the governance of their country. This right is embedded in the radical political changes that have taken place since the late nineteenth century, whereby most countries became republics and most kingdoms submitted themselves to some kind of constitutional and parliamentarian control. Moreover, almost all countries have enshrined rights and freedoms of their people in their constitutions. That means that, at least on paper, almost every state in the world adheres to the precept of governance by the people, for the people and of the people. And while reality can be quite different, this clearly did not deter millions of people worldwide to take to the streets to claim a restoration of their sovereignty in matters of state.

> **Sovereignty of the people**
>
> Of the 193 member states in the United Nations, 159 states call themselves 'republic', 17 call themselves 'kingdom' and the other 17 states use names like emirates, sultanates, states, princedoms, duchy. Only 9 countries use 'democratic' in their official name, although most of these are not deemed democratic in practice.
>
> *(These figures date from 2024 and are subject to change as states regularly change their official name)*

Elections

One way to give expression to the sovereignty of the people are elections. In the 1990s, the world witnessed a whole series of first-time national elections in countries all over the world. Western countries as well as the United Nations and the European Union aided these elections by convincing governments to hold them, by providing practical and financial assistance with the logistics, and by sending election observers to monitor them. However, elections were not sufficient to buttress democratic governments. First, because many an autocratic regime managed to either rigg the elections or implement election laws that prevented full participation. The resulting election victory allowed them to claim that they were elected as the leader of a functioning democracy even though everyone knew that the reality was different. The other problem was that elections do not make a democracy. A democracy is a system of checks and balances that gives the majority vote the right to govern during a given period of time while maintaining the rule of law that guarantees certain rights and freedoms for everyone. Autocratic regimes, after winning the electoral vote, used their democratic mandate to rule as they wished.

Civil society

Another approach undertaken in the 1990s to enhance democracy, was the notion of civil society. It was argued that a democracy can only function if government maintains a continuous conversation with the population. For this to function, it was considered best if people are organized in parties, unions, societies, organizations, churches, communities, clubs. These organizations generate discussions among the population that, in turn, can fuel the decision-making processes of governmental institutions of the state. In addition to elections whereby the population has the opportunity every so many years to express its political preferences, civil society is a means to stay in continuous dialogue with the government.

The concept of civil democracy provided a new approach to states and governance: rather than the top-down approach of governments telling people what to do, civil society is the bottom-up approach that ideally gives people more sovereignty in governance. In the 1990s, it was argued that most dictatorial regimes lacked a functioning civil society, either because the state had become the guiding power, as was the case in most communist and socialist countries, or because dictators had assumed all power. Even if they were overthrown and replaced by a democratic system, so the argument went, such a democracy could not function without a thriving civil society. The advocates of civil society saw their reasoning justified in the collapse of so many countries after their regimes had been overthrown: the social movements that had achieved the downfall of their regimes did not have the organization to install and uphold a democracy, and the society of these countries clearly lacked the infrastructure for supporting a democracy. To make sure that newly installed democracies are successful, the reasoning went, a civil society must be formed prior to the downfall of a regime.

It was mostly Western societies that adhered to this view, and from the 1990s onwards they started to invest in civil-society-building in countries that were considered undemocratic. While civil-society-partners on the ground often welcomed this support, the regimes saw it as foreign intervention meant to undermine the state. The countermeasures – penalizing the acceptance of foreign funds or the cooperation with foreign representatives – were usually effective in thwarting the efforts to build civil society in these countries. But even if the civil society efforts were successful, the bottom-up approach of civil society only rarely managed to permeate into the echelons of the state structure.

Democracy-building: Germany and Japan versus Iraq and Afghanistan

After the Second World War, the United States was instrumental in reshaping Japan and Germany into functioning democracies. Similar efforts in Afghanistan (2001-2004) and Iraq (2003-2004) failed completely, however. Scholars are still trying to understand the reasons why:

"The sharp ethnic and religious differences that divide the Iraqi and Afghani peoples are key impediments to the success of the current efforts to develop and sustain fully democratic political institution." (Andrew J. Enterline and J. Michael Greig Source, 'Against All Odds? The History of Imposed Democracy and the Future of Iraq and Afghanistan', *Foreign Policy Analysis*, 2008).

"Among other things, it is the level of forethought and preparedness and levelheadedness revealed by the administrator-training program in 1943 that made the nation-building and democratization experiments in Japan and Germany after 1945 so successful. And it is, I fear, the level of unpreparedness and muddleheadedness that (…) puts at great risk the experiments with nation-building and democratization in Iraq and Afghanistan." (Stanley Nide Katz, 'Democratic Constitutionalism after Military Occupation: Reflections on the United States' Experience in Japan, Germany, Afghanistan, and Iraq', *Common Knowledge*, 2006)

Good governance

The unsuccessful results of the civil-society approach of the 1990s and later, led to new views on what is essential in a democracy. For instance, could it be that 'state society' was neglected too much by overemphasizing 'civil society'? In other words, maybe the most effective way of transforming a state into a democracy would be top-down rather than bottom-up. This is when the concept of 'good governance' was introduced. Good governance takes a broad view on governance, which should not be limited to political governance, but also include social and economic wellbeing. Because of its broad meaning, there are many definitions that emphasize one or the other aspect of what good governance should be.

Looking back, it is surprising that these two concepts, good governance and civil society, were not discussed in conjunction, as they are complementary. But for a long time they led separate lives, being promoted by separate actors and agencies. Civil society was the domain of policy makers active in politics, while good governance was the domain of policymakers active in development work, and these two domains hardly interacted. Nowadays, the combination of both concepts is considered important to human wellbeing in general, as will be discussed in the chapter 'Sustainable Development'.

While the notion of good governance may receive international approval, it was mostly promoted by Western countries. This had a paradoxical effect. On the one hand, it reinforced the image and position of the state, allowing dictatorial types to stay in power in exchange for promises to improve their governance. On the other hand, the dictates made by Western countries in exchange for money would contribute to the increasing rift between what would become known as the global North and global South.

'Good governance'
The most cited definition has come from the United Nations which explains good governance on the basis of eight characteristics: it should be participatory, consensus oriented, accountable, transparent, responsive, effective and efficient, equitable and inclusive, and in accordance with the rule of law.

World Bank
The notion of 'good governance' was the brainchild of international donor agencies, particularly the World Bank. Between 2002-2007, the World Bank loaned US$ 23 billion for projects related to good governance.

Further reading

Merilee Serrill Grindle, "Good Governance: The Inflation of An Idea", Harvard Kennedy School, CID Working Paper No. 202, October 2010

Samuel P. Huntington, *The Third Wave: Democratization in the Late Twentieth Century*, University of Oklahoma Press, 1993

Donavon Johnson (ed.), *Rethinking Democracy and Governance. Perspectives from the Caribbean*, Routledge, 2024

Haroon A. Khan, *The Idea of Good Governance and the Politics of the Global South. An Analysis of its Effects*, Routledge, 2016

Munyaradzi Mawere and Tendai R Mwanaka (eds.), *Democracy, Good Governance and Development in Africa*, Langaa RPCID, 2015

Surendra Munshi and Biju Paul Abraham (eds.), *Good Governance, Democratic Societies and Globalisation*, SAGE Publications India Pvt Ltd, 2004

World Bank, "Governance and Development" World Bank, 1992

CHAPTER 7

Human rights

Agreements on prosperity or on peace are of all ages and therefore constitute a global structure. International agreements on values, on the other hand, are relatively new and represent a global trend. This is particularly the case with human rights, that received global acceptance in the second half of the 20th century and then gained global traction in the 1990s. However, this did not mean that human rights were embraced everywhere. On the contrary, many countries were quite reluctant to do so. Nevertheless, human rights became a global trend because it was a discourse almost all countries felt they needed to relate to, whether wholeheartedly or not.

Agreeing on international values: freedom and human rights

A quick scan of international agreements about values shows that they are usually about justice, freedom, human rights and equality (peace is also often mentioned, but that is not a value but a state of affairs.) One of the key characteristics of these values is that they usually lack clear definitions. They are easy to use, they can evoke strong emotions and they can make people take to the streets and start revolutions, but it is very difficult to provide accurate descriptions of them. People are willing to fight for justice, for example, but when asked what exactly they mean by that, the answer will be either vague ('no oppression') or short-term ('this government must go').

One of the values that people (and states) have managed to make tangible, is **freedom**. We distinguish between two types of freedom. One is the freedom to be allowed to do something, like voicing an opinion or professing to a religion. The other freedom is the freedom not to having to suffer from certain things, like censorship, oppression, torture or poverty. In the English language these two types are known as the freedom *of* something, and the freedom *from* something. More so than the notion of justice, these ideas about freedom could be translated into workable concepts. By the second half of the 20th century, they became the centerpiece of one of the most influential value systems of our times: human rights.

The origins of human rights are debated. Muslims and Christians claim that the fundamental rights of men are already present in their holy scriptures, the Chinese and the Africans say the same about their ancient civilizations, and the Americans and the French will argue that they were the first to write it down in constitutions. The human rights discussed here are those enshrined in international agreements that were endorsed by most states. The first of these agreements was not a treaty but the (non-binding) Universal Declaration of Human Rights (1948). This declaration was later criticized for being drafted by mostly Western countries at a time when three quarters of the other states had yet to gain their independence. However, the binding human rights treaties were drafted much later and also included the input of many other states.

The human rights of these treaties are organized in legal terms in which two important elements stand out. First, human rights are freedoms that people – individuals or communities – can invoke against their state. Second, human rights are divided into two types. **Classical (or political) rights** are freedoms in which the state should not interfere: the government should not dictate what religion should be, what ideas should be allowed and what ideas shouldn't, and what organizations should be allowed and which shouldn't. **Social rights**, on the other hand, are freedoms that should be actively enabled and guaranteed by the state, like education, housing, nutrition. In other words, these two sets of freedoms demand opposite roles of the state: classical freedoms require the state to stand back, social freedoms to step in.

Declaration of Human Duties and Responsibilities (HDR), 1998

This non-binding declaration was drafted by experts, philosophers, artists and Nobel laureates in response to the Universal Declaration of Human Rights of 1948. For these human rights to not only be recognized but also implemented, the drafters of the HDR argued, there must be a duty and responsibility on all people and authorities to do so.

The global trend of human rights

Even though the main human rights treaties were active since the 1960s, human rights ony became a global trend from the 1990s onwards. At the 1993 United Nations Conference on Human Rights in Vienna, governments from almost all states in the world voted to reaffirm the universality of human rights and there was a proliferation of international non-state actors whose goal it was to promote human rights. In most Western states, human rights became an important part of their national and foreign policy, and large sums were spent on the promotion and endorsement of human rights in the world.

By the late 1990s however, the momentum of this global push for human rights started to falter. Several factors played a role. One was that human rights were championed primarily by Western states. They made it a condition for trade or other cooperation agreements with states that had a bad human rights track record. Human rights standards had to be met for such agreements to be implemented. This conditionality may have served the world-wide endorsement of human rights, but the targeted states did not look favorably upon this method, partly because some of these states were ruled by dictators who were violating human rights and were not willing to change their ways, and partly because it was reminiscent of colonial times with these same Western nations acting like the colonial powers they used to be, imposing 'civilizational' dictates.

Another aspect that complicated human rights policies was terrorism. In the 1990s, several countries in the Middle East and Asia were suffering from terrorist attacks within their own societies. The response of the states to these attacks was often met with criticism from Western countries for being a violation of human rights. However, when the United States suffered the 9/11 attacks of 2001 and declared the 'war on terror', many of its antiterrorism measures were not unlike those they had criticized in other countries like military courts, incarceration without trial, 'enhanced' interrogation and extended powers for police and secret service agencies. A similar change in attitude emerged in Europe after the terrorist attacks that took place between 2004 and 2015.

The human rights trend also slowed due to debates about its purpose. While human rights and democracy were seen as the ideal path to peace and development everywhere in the early 1990s, this view faced growing criticism. The premise of the human rights agenda is that a society which respects and promotes individual freedoms is more likely to enjoy economic growth than one in which collective or state rights supercede civil or political freedom. The counter argument was that there is little use endorsing human rights if basic social and economic living conditions are not addressed first. The question then was whether economic and social rights (as enshrined in the 1966 International Covenant on Economic, Social and Cultural Rights) should take prevalence over human rights, or vice versa. This principled discussion turned into a stalemate between Western countries on the one hand, and most of the other countries in the world on the other hand. In the meantime, several states, especially in East and Southeast Asia, made significant economic progress without meeting international human rights standards, thereby negating the premise that human rights are conditional to economic prosperity.

As the human rights agenda of the 1990s gradually became dormant in the 2010s, it was usurped by the new global concept of 'human security' which will be discussed in more detail in the Chapter 'Security'.

Has the global situation of human rights improved since the 1990s?

This question is hard to answer, mainly because it is difficult to qualify the 'improvement' of human rights. A perusal of international human rights reports suggests that the upholding of political and civil rights have been in decline since the 1990s. Women's rights had seen a steady improvement since the 1970s, but progress appears to be slowing down since the 2010s.

Criticisms

Even though human rights may have lost their high status on the international political agenda, there is still a consensus among all states on the need for and importance of human rights. However, different views have emerged regarding the interpretation of human rights.

The first form of criticism has to do with the premise that each **individual** human being is entitled to human rights. Especially countries in Asia and Africa consider this a typical Western approach. They argue that in their societies it is not the individual, but the **community** that has prevalence. The individual has rights, they argue, but these do not always trump those of the family, the village, the clan or the nation at large. These countries do furthermore believe that the individual approach to human rights as we know today, does not entirely fit the needs and principles of these societies.

The second criticism challenges the notion of **universality of human rights**. It argues that the human rights as framed in most of the early treaties are essentially Western constructs that deny other perspectives. This criticism is known as **cultural relativism**, which claims that values should always be seen and weighed in their cultural context. In the 1990s, 'Socialist', 'Islamic' and 'African' human rights emerged as alternative views. It can be argued that these discussions were also very political, pitting the 'global South' against the 'global North'.

The third type of criticism is the accusation that Western countries maintain **double standards** in upholding international human rights law. This criticism peaked in 2023-2025 with the war and ensuing humanitarian crisis in Gaza. The International Court of Justice and the International Criminal Court considered the Israeli response to a large-scale Hamas attack in violation of international humanitarian and human rights regulations. The fact that many Western states were unwilling to uphold these charges against Israel was considered by other states to be typical of Western double standards when applying human rights law. This situation would fuel the already growing disgruntlement of the global South vis-à-vis the global North.

Human rights and state sovereignty: the Nuremberg and Tokyo trials (1946-1948)
State sovereignty dictates that people are only accountable to their national laws. According to this legal logic, the leaders and military of Japan and Germany during the Second World War could not be held accountable for crimes as long as their actions were lawful under their own laws. The international criminal tribunals of Nuremberg and Tokyo broke with this legal principle: human rights – in this case framed as 'crimes against humanity' – could override state sovereignty.

Further reading

Jack Donnelly, *Universal Human Rights in Theory and Practice*, Cornell University Press, 2013

Michael Ignatieff, *Human Rights as Politics and Idolatry*, Princeton University Press, 2000

Samuel Moyn, *The Last Utopia: Human Rights in History*, The Belknap Press, 2012

Aryeh Neier, *The International Human Rights Movement: A History*, Princeton University Press, 2020

Christopher Roberts, *Alternative Approaches to Human Rights. The Disparate Historical Paths of the European, Inter-American and African Regional Human Rights Systems*, Cambridge University Press, 2022

Susan Waltz, 'Reclaiming and rebuilding the history of the Universal Declaration of Human Rights', *Third World Quarterly*, 2002, Vol. 23 No. 3, pp. 437-448

PART IV
Global Challenges

A global challenge is a particularly problematic issue on a global scale that affects people worldwide and that requires concerted efforts by various actors to be addressed. Global challenges can be very diverse in nature. Examples include climate change, migration, resource scarcity, security and sustainable development. We will discuss a selection of seven global challenges in the following chapters.

While global *problems* may often be recognized as such, they only become a global *challenge* when a large part of the international community declares that concerted efforts are needed to address it. An example is climate change which was already marked as a global problem by scholars in the 1960s but only became recognized as a global challenge in the 2000s. Conversely, global problems may be denied the status of global challenge, like during the Covid-19-pandemic of 2019-2022 when some state leaders denied its lethal nature calling it a form of flu and consequently saw no need for international cooperation to combat this disease. And then there are certain global events that may be declared a global challenge even if that status is disputed. This has been the case with terrorism ('global war on terror') and with migration: in both instances, critics argued that these issues may indeed have global proportions, but that they don't qualify as a global challenge because they are not as globally threatening as politicians make them out to be.

> **Challenge multiplier**
> Global challenges are usually not caused by a single, but by numerous problematic issues. Sometimes they compound each other and become challenge multipliers: for instance, a region that is suffering under a civil war (or famine or climate change) may cause migration which may cause health problems that can lead to a pandemic.

Nexus

Global challenges are usually composed of several global problems and even if they don't always seem related, they are often interconnected or even serve as multipliers. Such a cluster of issues and influences is called a nexus. One of the first steps in addressing a global challenge is to identify its nexuses. For instance, if migration is considered a challenge for a certain region, different approaches can be taken to address that challenge, with each approach creating its own set of nexuses. If the approach is to physically stop the influx of migrants, this creates a nexus of security. This nexus, in turn, fans out into several other nexuses, like border policing or cutting deals with neighboring countries, deals that may include taking in migrants in exchange for financial compensation. If, on the other hand, the approach to the challenge of migration is to address the causes of migration, this creates the nexus of foreign policy. Since the causes of migration can be multiple (civil war, lack of economic prospects, natural disasters, political persecution), the foreign policy nexus fans out in various other nexuses, each related to one of these – apparently unrelated – issues.

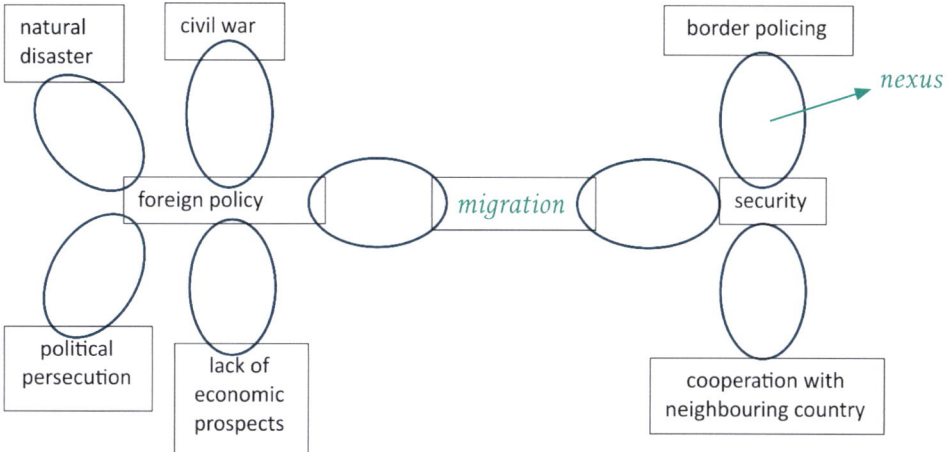

Figure IV.0.1 Nexus 'migration'

Nexus

A nexus is the mutual influence between issues that belong to different domains and therefore seem unrelated. Global challenges often contain one or more nexuses that need to be addressed to reach a solution.

CHAPTER 1

Information and communication

Communication – or the exchange of information – is essential to the existence of human beings. It is the lubricant that keeps the global structures, trends and challenges going. Communication takes on many forms: arts, language, music, signs and symbols. Language is a vital element of communication, not only to exchange information, but also to frame realities. Saying that someone has 'died' or was 'killed', 'murdered' or 'exterminated' makes difference. Similarly, the style and rhetoric used in language has great influence on people. Advertisers know that, and so do politicians and propagandists.

Since the early 2000s, advances in communication technology, especially in terms of the internet and social media, have intensified communication on a global scale in numerous ways. Following the telegraph and telephone in the late nineteenth century came the internet and the mobile phone in the late twentieth century, and the smartphone and social media since the early 2000s. These developments contributed to the advancement and improvement of human life. But they also pose challenges because of misuse and negative effects. While misinformation and propaganda have always been part of human communication, the scale it has reached today poses several problems on a global scale. Whether these problems also pose a 'global challenge' as defined in this textbook– that is: concerted global efforts are required to deal with the problem – remains to be seen. But people and governments across the world are struggling with the ways these technologies are used and the effects they have.

Recent technological innovations in communication:

Internet: invented in 1983, popularized in 1990s

Facebook: 2004

iPhone: 2007

Instagram: 2010

ChatGPT: 2023

Worldwide access to internet

In 2024, the number of internet users world-wide stood at 5.44 billion, which means that around two-thirds of the global population was connected to the internet. The highest percentage of users was in Northern Europe (97%), the highest number of users was in China (1 billion).

(Statista.com, 2024)

Facts and fiction

Age limit to mobile phones?

Neurologists and psychiatrists have pointed at the negative effects of mobile phone use, especially among children and young adults. Some of those effects are mental (anxiety, depression, sleeping disorders) or social (problems in initiating and maintaining social relations). For that reason, more and more schools across the world are restricting or even banning the mobile phone.

Scholars of the Natural Sciences pride themselves on dealing with facts. But we have seen that this is more complex in the Humanities, the academic discipline that underpins International Studies. Students of International Studies are expected to base their findings on empirical observation but they must also try to understand what is happening, why and how. We can use the existence of God as an example. While the academics may argue that the existence of God cannot be empirically proven, the believers may find their belief in God's existence doesn't require empirical proof. The student of Humanities, in turn, may dismiss such belief as unscientific but must also inquire into the how and why of this belief. To do so in an academically sound manner requires the use of various methods and theories (see chapter 'Multi- and Inter-disciplinarity'). This is how the academic world tries to create clarity in the realms of fact, fiction and belief.

There is a problem, however, when such distinctions are not being made. For example, when a proven fact is considered mere fiction, or the reverse, when fiction is presented as proven fact that needs no further empirical proof. Climate change or the effect of vaccination may be empirically proven by natural scientists, but for some people that proof is not a reason to believe it is true. They see these scientific facts as mere fiction and may present their own and different beliefs as factual truths. **'Knowledge resistance'** is the term for the denial of widely accepted scientific facts in favor of alternative ideas.

From an academic perspective, this reversal of fact and fiction is problematic even though this is nothing new in other domains: politicians and advertisers have known for centuries that selling a message is more important than its factual content, and that bending the truth may sometimes be needed to make people believe that message. But social media and the possibility of creating deep-fakes have amplified this human behavior on a massive and global scale. It shows how important the act of believing is in human interactions, but at the same time presents students of Humanities (and therefore International Studies) with a considerable challenge.

This chapter will highlight three mechanisms that play a role in these processes of fact-versus-fiction and that are relevant to International Studies: framing, public diplomacy and conspiracy theories.

Framing

Studies that focus on media, communication, politics and literature have developed various theories that help explain the ways in which messages are conveyed. One of these is called Framing Theory. According to this theory, statements made by people do not have meaning in and of themselves but only acquire meaning in the context (the 'frame') in which they are used. For instance, the statement "color has no meaning to me", means something entirely different when said in a discussion on the choice of paint than it does in a discussion on race. And if the latter was said immediately after the abolition of apartheid in South Africa it may have been considered positive (because it may appeal to the notion of the rainbow nation indicating that the color of your skin makes no difference) but not so in the context of Black Lives Matter.

An important role in framing is played by the people involved in the exchange messages. Framing Theory distinguishes between four parties: between those who make statements and those who are addressed, and between insiders and outsiders. For instance, talking about religion has a different impact on believers than on non-believers. A sermon about the Holy Scripture will make little sense to those who were not raised in that faith, and it will mean something different still to those who have studied it but do not belong to the faith it represents.

Framing is happening all the time, intentionally as well as unintentionally. It happens unintentionally when, for instance, we are joking or insulting each other. Unconsciously we are aware of the right frame for the intended audience and purpose, for instance to make others laugh about the joke or be offended by the insult. If the framing is incorrect however, people may laugh at the insult, be offended by the joke, or just raise their eyebrows. Framing also happens intentionally. Politicians, activists, ideologues, advertisers, influencers and all those who want to convey their message to others will be keenly aware of how they frame that message, and they will probably change the framing when addressing different audiences.

Public and cultural diplomacy

Diplomacy is the maintaining of relationships among states on a governmental level. Diplomats, as representatives of one state, maintain contacts with their counterparts of the other state where they are posted. Nowadays, however, states have become increasingly aware that the perception that people abroad have of their country, matters. If the United States spends a great deal of money on infrastructure and development aid in any given country but is nevertheless perceived by the people of that country as an imperialist bully, then something is amiss in America's foreign policy image. For that policy to be effective, it is argued, it must not only focus on the relationship between governments but also on trying to understand the people and society of that other country and perhaps even on trying to influence these people rather than their government. This is what has become known as public diplomacy. One of the first initiatives to develop such policy was taken by the United States after the attacks of 9/11 in 2001. It was inspired by the realization that a large part of the Muslim world resented the United States and this resulted in an American rethinking of its foreign policy in a report with the title *Changing hearts, winning peace*.

> **Public diplomacy** is a part of foreign policy that a) aims at enhancing the state's image abroad by b) actively targeting the public rather than the government of a foreign country, with c) a variety of activities and messages.

Public and cultural diplomacy

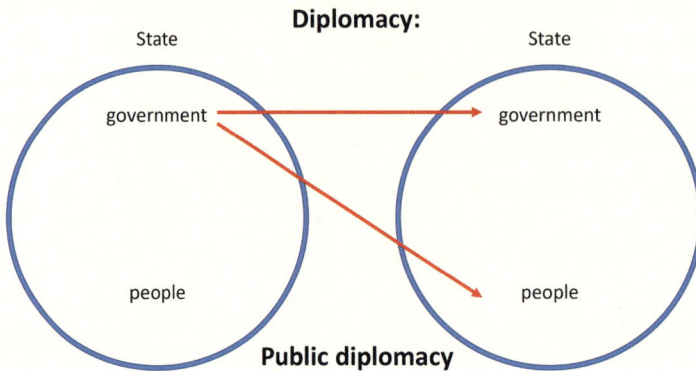

Figure IV.1.1 Public and cultural diplomacy

A subsection of public diplomacy is **cultural diplomacy**. This type of diplomacy deliberately avoids the topic of politics and aims for countries to meet on a common, less controversial ground. This is usual the domain of culture or sports. Most countries apply cultural diplomacy on an incidental basis, for instance by having their embassies organize concerts by musicians from their home country. Some countries have permanent cultural representation abroad, like the United Kingdom (*British Council*), France (*Alliance Française*), Spain (*Instituto Cervantes*) and Germany (*Goethe Institute*). A newcomer in this field is China that for a long time pursued its foreign policies without caring much about its image abroad, but this has changed. It has established the Division for Public Diplomacy as part of the Ministry of Foreign Affairs, rapidly expanded the *Confucius Institutes* around the world, and the Chinese state news agency has a growing number of foreign-language news outlets.

These types of foreign policy are typical forms of soft power. Since the early 2000s, there has been a steep rise in the deployment of this kind of soft power around the world. However, at the same time there was also an increase in so-called sharp power, whereby state-organized centers disseminate false information to influence public opinion in other countries.

These developments show that countries – especially the larger states – see an urgent need for influencing the public opinion abroad, and they do so for different reasons and with a variety of friendly and aggressive means.

Conspiracy theory

The basic framework of any conspiracy is that people work in secret behind the scenes to achieve a certain goal. However, the term conspiracy is used in two ways. One is the secret plot to kill the king, overthrow a regime, start an uprising. History is rife with such plots and some are uncovered or fail in their execution, while others succeed (see text box). The other usage of the term 'conspiracy theory' is usually reserved for something that is much grander in terms of conspirators, the scale of their intent, and the means employed. In this scenario, the conspirators are not made up of a small band of angry anarchists or grumbling generals but are deeply embedded in the state or are made up of secret societies with a global network. Their goal is power, preferably world power. And the means of reaching that goal are either by deception or by creating chaos through violence. The massive vaccination campaigns against the Covid-19 virus are an example of what was perceived as such a plot: it was said that government elites were inoculating entire populations with substances that would submit them to the will of that elite.

Famous secret plots that were uncovered

In 1605, a plot known as the Gunpowder Conspiracy was uncovered with the intention to blow up the Houses of Parliament in London. In 1953, the CIA conspired (and succeeded) in overthrowing the government of Iranian prime minister Mosaddeq who was considered too leftist. In 2016, a massive creation of Russian false accounts was uncovered on American social media that were spreading false information, ostensibly to influence the upcoming elections. In 2022, a large and eclectic group of people in Germany known under the name of Reichsbürger movement was arrested on the charge of conspiring to overthrow the government and establish a new regime in Germany.

Conspiracy theories of the second type are of all times, but they appear to have increased in popularity since the 2010s. Some scholars have argued that the number of conspiracy theories are not higher than before, but that they are merely disseminated and multiplied more due to social media. Whatever the exact causes, the phenomenon of conspiracy theories does coincide with the development of increasingly blurry lines between fact and fiction.

A typical feature of most of these conspiracy theories is that it is usually hard to prove that they are not true. How do we disprove that man did *not* land on the moon, that the attack on the Twin Towers in 9/11 was *not* orchestrated by the CIA, that a university professor is *not* a member of the Illuminati? From an academic point of view, there is little use in disproving what is already generally accepted as empirical proof. Something much more relevant to students of International Studies however, are the 'why' and 'how' questions: *why* do people turn to such theories, and *how* do such theories impact societies? This line of inquiry leads to two questions: why are conspiracy theories so popular and how do they work?

Popular 'conspiracy theories'

Illuminati: a secret society of elite professionals – doctors, politicians, judges – who control the world.

Reptile humanoids: an alien species has landed on earth and has gradually taken over the ruling elites with the aim to subdue the human species to slavery.

Lady Diana: the car accident was a set-up by the British Royal Palace to get rid of her.

Flat Earth: scientists make us believe that the earth is a sphere while in fact it is a disc.

Popularity

The study of conspiracy theories is ongoing and quite inconclusive due to their elusive nature. Scholars usually steer away from ascertaining what is fact and what is fiction and try to understand the underlying mechanisms. The main characteristic that all conspiracy theories have in common is that 'something is out there that wants to get us'. Such convictions combine the feeling of being threatened and a sense of powerlessness against that threat. Other features of conspiracy theories are a fear of the unknown, a distrust of government or any international governing body, a sense of helplessness and, consequently, self-victimization. These sentiments are in themselves nothing new. They are typical of humankind throughout history. But since the 2010s these conspiracy sentiments have started to become more common and several developments may be conducive to this change. The first is that a period of relative global optimism which had started in the late 1980s (see chapter 'Democracy') was quickly succeeded by a period of uncertainty and deeply felt insecurity. Another development is the globalization of politics and economy, which may give people the impression that they are no longer in control of their own affairs. These developments may have contributed to a sense of powerlessness that, in turn, led to self-victimization: it is not we who are at fault, but others. Finally, these ideas and sentiments were amplified by social media technologies, which created a constant flow of (mis-)information that is unparalleled in human history.

Impact

The main impact of conspiracy theories seems to be the distrust of governments and elites who are suspected of hidden motives. Several conspiracy theories, like those of the 'reptile-humanoid' or the vaccination, hold that the government intends to control the people, and reduce them to obedient subjects. If such a conspiracy theory gains many followers, the distrust of a government may undermine the socio-political fabric of a society. Similarly, when the refusal to be vaccinated reaches a certain demographic percentage, this opens the way to a new outbreak of diseases that had been eradicated thanks to national vaccination programs.

Another impact of conspiracy theories can be the targeting of a specific group. In Europe, Jews have for centuries been accused of 'blood libel' (sacrificing Christian children) and since the nineteenth century they have become the object of the conspiracy theory claiming that Jews are part of a secret network that controls the world, financed by rich Jewish families. These theories have become embedded in antisemitism. Similarly, the so-called love jihad conspiracy theories that go around Hindu communities in India claim that Muslim men seduce Hindu women to convert them to Islam. And popular in Western countries is the so-called replacement theory, which holds that migrants – particularly those of color and non-Christian – may cause or even want white Christians to disappear.

Further reading

Michael Butter and Peter Knight (eds.), *Routledge Handbook of Conspiracy Theories*, Routledge, 2020.

Melvin L. DeFleur and Margaret H. DeFleur, 'Framing Theory' (chapter) in *Mass Communication Theories*, Routledge, 2022

Edward P. Djerejian (chairman Advisory Group on Public Diplomacy for the Arab and Muslim World), *Changing Minds Winning Peace. A new strategic direction for U.S. public diplomacy in the Arab & Muslim world*, Report submitted to the Committee on Appropriations, U.S. House of Representatives, October 1, 2003

J. Knight, J., 'Analysing Knowledge Diplomacy and Differentiating It from Soft Power and Cultural, Science, Education and Public Diplomacies,' *The Hague Journal of Diplomacy*, 18(4), 2022, pp.654-686.

CHAPTER 2

Sustainable Development

In 2015, the United Nations called sustainable development a global issue that needed concerted international effort to address. The elements that made up sustainable development as a global challenge had already long existed and had been recognized as such. The concept of sustainable development, however, presented an integrated view on several interconnected global problems that international actors could work with. Sustainable development, therefore, is a term that stands for a goal (this is what the world should strive for), a means (this is how it should be done), and a global challenge (to reach this goal and deploy the means, concerted efforts are needed).

From development aid to sustainable development

The precursor of sustainable development was **development aid**. This was the financial aid extended by rich countries to poor countries (later rephrased in the aid from 'developed' to 'underdeveloped' countries). This financial assistance has been motivated and criticized for a variety of reasons. Motivations for such aid was the argument by former colonized countries that the former colonizers had a debt to pay for their colonizing practices.

> ### Pros and cons of development aid
> "A constant stream of 'free' money is a perfect way to keep an inefficient or simply bad government in power. As aid flows in, there is nothing more for the government to do – it doesn't need to raise taxes, and as long as it pays its army, it doesn't have to take account off its disgruntled citizens."
> (Economist Dambisa Moyo in *Dead Aid: Why aid is not working and how there is a better way for Africa*, 2010).
>
> "Aid can help to build the free press, or support the training and recruitment of judges, civil society, and independent audit institutions. In fact, aid can play an important part in fighting corruption through generating public demand to end it."
> (Oxfam International, *Good Aid*, YouTube 23 April 2010)

Motivations from within 'developed' countries were often framed in terms of civic or religious (usually Christian) duty: fellow human beings needed to be helped. Critics argued that this aid was a continuation of colonization, whereby the 'developed' countries maintain control over the lifelines of 'developing' countries. Other critics pointed at the lack of success of this aid, which to them was a waste of or even the very reason that developing countries remained underdeveloped.

In the late 1980s, a change took place in the Western world in the way they looked at the world. This was allegedly prompted by the songs *Feed the World* and *Do They know it's Christmas* sung by a large group of top Western musicians, but the main cause was most likely the end of the Cold War with the collapse of the Soviet Union in 1991. Somehow, a general conviction emerged that it was not ideologies (communism, liberalism) that were important, but rather the wellbeing of humankind. Based on these ideas, the United Nations developed the ambitious project of the **Millennium Development Goals**. These were eight goals that were to be met in the first fifteen years of the new millennium, beginning in 2000 and ending by 2015. While this project still had the characteristics of development aid – rich countries gave bi-lateral financial assistance to poor countries – it was the first time that these endeavors were undertaken multilaterally and globally. This approach gave the project a sense of global urgency although the good intentions were not enough to reach the goals within the given time.

Millenium Development Goals (2000 - 2015)
1   Eradicate extreme poverty and hunger.
2   Achieve universal primary education.
3   Promote gender equality and empower women.
4   Reduce child mortality.
5   Improve maternal health.
6   Combat HIV/AIDS, malaria and other diseases.
7   Ensure environmental sustainability.
8   Global partnership for development.

For that reason, a new set of goals was agreed for the next fifteen years. These were the **Sustainable Development Goals**, as agreed by the United Nations, and they were to be met by 2030. The Sustainable Development goals were not just a continuation of the Millennium goals, they were instead a different concept entirely. It was recognized that everything was related to human well-being was interconnected, so that help in one area would be of little use if other areas were not also addressed. So, for instance, when donors bring in agricultural equipment to work the fields, but there are no trained mechanics to repair this equipment, then within several years this equipment becomes useless. Or one can help a village increase its fruit production, but to make that profitable they need roads and trucks to move it out, and to build these roads one may run into corrupt government officials. Or one may provide pumps to drill for more wells but if this means a depletion of ground water, then in the long run the land will be unfit for agriculture, and its erosion will affect all nearby lands. From these experiences grew the realization that all issues of development are interrelated and therefore need an interrelated approach.

Sustainable development goals (simplified):

What is to be sustained:
Nature: Earth, Biodiversity, Ecosystems
Life support: Ecosystem, Resources, Environment
Community: Cultures, Groups, Places

What is to be developed:
People: Life expectancy, Education, Equity, Equal opportunity
Economy: Wealth, Productive sectors, Consumption
Society: Institutions, Social capital, States, Regions

From all these ideas and experiences grew the realization that these sustainable development goals were targets not only for a few countries, but for the entire world. This was not a new idea. Ever since the 1970s, several informal societies of politicians and scientists had come up with similar ideas and visions. But now the ideas were turned into policy globally.

Indicators and targets

A practical problem that faces these optimistic endeavors is the confusion about terminology, data, and measurement. How do we measure the success of reaching sustainable development goals? Basically, this is done by means of targets and indicators. The **targets** are the Sustainable Development Goals. The **indicators** are how one measures. Most indicators that measure the success rate of sustainable development activities use some form of quantification: the radio program promoting democracy has had forty hours of airtime, the minimum income in that country has gone up by five percent, a hundred more people in this town have access to clean water. Numbers are an easy way to measure things, but they are not always suitable for a given situation. For instance, poverty is usually measured on the basis of income, and the standard of extreme poverty is set by the World Bank to an income of less than one dollar a day. However, while some communities that have been living in forests all their lives might meet that standard, they do not necessarily live in extreme poverty, as is perhaps the case for people in cities with five or ten dollars a day.

It is therefore recognized that these indicators do not always reflect the reality of the targets. For many academics it is reason to avoid using them as much as possible (although many cannot find it hard resist this quantitative approach) and try to find different measurement methods. Policymakers, by contrast, prefer to work with targets and using quantitative indicators is a practical means to show whether and how much progress is being made.

The actors

While the policy framework of the Sustainable Development Goals was mostly decided by states, the NGOs (both local and international) do the implementation. These two actors have an intertwined relationship: NGOs are active in the field and are therefore often consulted by the states in developing policies, and the NGOs are largely dependent on the states for the funding of their activities. This creates an interdependent relationship that may sometimes lead to questions about the independence of NGOs (see chapter 'Non-state actors').

A special role is reserved for NGOs with a religious background ('Faith-based organizations'). In the world of sustainable development, their activities and positions in society are often overlooked by mostly secular policy makers. This might be because many FBOs do not need state funding because they have their own resources for that, or because secular states often do not want to accommodate the religious agenda of these organizations and therefore don't grand them funding. However, it has been argued that collaboration with FBOs might be advisable because they are often much deeper and broader embedded in civil society than secular NGOs and they may have alternative views on sustainable development that can be more effective, especially among the religious communities.

World Bank and FBOs

In 1998, Jim Wolfensohn, President of the World Bank, and Lord Carey, the Archbishop of Canterbury and the leader of the English Anglican Church, took the initiative to establish the World Faiths Development Dialogue, a platform which continues until today in supporting faith-based organizations in their work among the very poor.

Human development

Development and development aid as we knew it from the 1960s through the 1980s was generally seen in economic terms. A country's development was expressed in terms of Gross Domestic Product, the calculated total of private consumption, business investments, government spending and net exports. But this definition and measurement of development did not hold. The measuring stick of **economic growth** was gradually replaced by that of **fulfilled lives**. This new category measured in terms of a healthy life, a good education, a meaningful job, family life, democratic state structures, and so on.

Measuring development in terms of people's lives is called **human development**. This approach is multi-dimensional and plural. Human development is about education as much as about health and about culture as much as about political participation. It deals with fiscal policy as much as health policy, with educational policy as much as gender policy or environmental, industrialization or technological policy. And so on and so forth. In short, human development relates to many aspects that concern people's lives, not only economic ones. It can therefore not be put within a single academic discipline because it encompasses many, including economics, law, sociology, political science, environmental studies, urban studies and philosophy.

The concepts

A key notion in the conceptualization of human development is the **capability approach** which argues that the goal of development should be that people must have the capability of making a fulfilled life for themselves. This capability is expressed by some as the **freedom** to promote or achieve goals that are considered valuable. By others it is expressed in terms of **choices**: development should aim at expanding people's choices, for instance by means of improved healthcare and education, so that people are more capable of achieving their development goals. The capability approach has triggered an interesting discussion. Because what are responsible uses of freedom, what are valuable choices? Is that to be decided by every individual, regardless of how reprehensible, ill-informed, or harmful they may be in their actions? Or should the state interfere, for the sake of the general well-being? For example, if people from a rich country value their annual vacation and prefer to travel abroad, should the state then give them the opportunities to do so cheaply by deregulating air travel and allowing budget airlines to operate? Or should these choices be restricted because air travel is a significant contributor to climate change, with disastrous effects on the lives of current and future generations, especially among the poor?

Thinkers of human development

The great thinkers about human development are all from Asia. **Amartya Sen** (India, 1933) is one of the great inspirational thinkers about human development and this won him the Nobel Prize in Economic Sciences in 1998. **Mahbub ul-Haq** (Pakistan, 1934-1998) provided the practical framework to put human development into action. **Mohammed Yunus** (Bangladesh, 1940) developed the notion of micro-finance, which won him the Nobel Peace Prize in 2006. **Seyyed Hossein Nasr** (Iran, 1933) is a leading thinker on the spiritual dimensions of human development.

This brings us to another key notion in human development: **agency**. This term means that people are their own masters: they are the ones who decide, act, move, think. Only when people have full agency, will they be able to make the choices needed to improve their lives. For many, therefore, the overarching goal of human development should be to enable people's agency. Only then can they reach the second goal, which is their well-being.

The implementation

The challenge was to put these great ideas into practice. For this, the Pakistani economist Mahbub ul-Haq developed four indicators that are now widely used when implementing policies of human development.

The first indicator is *equity*. This refers to the concept of justice, impartiality and fairness (see chapter 'Equality and Self-determination'). The principle of equity is to create a level playing field of equal opportunity. This may require preferential treatment or affirmative action for those who do not have the same opportunities due to various disadvantages they face, thereby leveling the playing field.

The second is *efficiency*: this means the optimal use of existing resources. This is perhaps the most economics-oriented of these indicators, because efficiency is to maximize opportunities for individuals and communities through optimal use of human, material and institutional resources at the lowest cost. It sounds logical if you think about it, but efficiency has always been, and still remains, a challenge for societies.

The third indicator is *participation and empowerment*: in the human development approach, people are both the ends as well as the means to development.

Empowerment is needed to make the motor of agency work, because only then can people start participating and make life decisions. This principle may sound very social but is very political. Because it implies that people need to be involved at every stage of decision-making processes in their societies. They are not merely the beneficiaries of a state, but act as agents that make society function. This is where the notion of civil society emerges.

The fourth and final indicator is *sustainability*: The term sustainability is often used to refer to the environment, but it also encompasses social and economic dimensions. The notion of sustainability as used here, demands that all these dimensions are addressed together in a comprehensive manner. Only this way, so it is argued, can we reach a degree of human development that is not incidental but enduring.

It must be noted that these ideas still need to be worked out in practice. Ideally, all these concepts and indicators are implemented in a joint manner. But to actually do that is precisely the challenge.

Further reading

Tomáš Hák, Svatava Janoušková, Bedřich Moldan, 'Sustainable Development Goals: A need for relevant indicators', *Ecological Indicators*, Vol. 60, 2016, pp. 565-573

Walter Leal Filho (ed.), *Handbook of Sustainability Science and Research*, Springer 2018

Ortrud Lessmann and Felix Rauschmayer (eds.), *The Capability Approach and Sustainability*, Routledge 2014

Riley Quinn, *An Analysis of Mahbub ul Haq's Reflections on Human Development*, Maqat Library, 2017

United Nations, *Transforming our World: The 2030 Agenda for Sustainable Development*, 2015 (online publication)

CHAPTER 3

Resources and climate

Access to basic resources is one of the main interests of people. Water for drinking and farming, wood and oil for fuel, iron and stone for making tools and constructing buildings. With the advancement of technology, the need for more varied resources increased. Oil only became a prime interest from the 1920s onwards, when steam engines were replaced by engines working on diesel. The gradual replacement of oil by electricity since the 2010s increased the interest in rare ores like coltan and lithium, which were of little relevance until then but were now needed for batteries. Even if one were to argue that people today could very well do without a car or a mobile phone, these items are considered vital to the lives of human beings (see chapter 'Economy'), and consequently one is willing to go through great lengths and costs to gain access to the resources to produce them. It shows that the concept of 'essential needs' is subject to interpretation and depends on time and circumstance. Consequently, the resulting dependency on certain resources shapes the behavior of people, companies, and states.

> **Human considerations in changing resources**
> The shifts from the use of wood to coal to oil in the 19th and 20th century are usually explained in terms of technological improvement. But there were also social considerations. Water mills could have provided the necessary energy for the English industrialization in the nineteenth century, but the steam engine gave manufacturers more freedom: they did not have to negotiate intricate property rights to access running water, and they could set up their mills close to the labourers in urban centres. Social considerations also played a role in the move from coal (needed to produce steam) to oil: oil exploitation far away did not cause social unrest as was the case with the coalminers close at home.
> (Andreas Malm, The Origins of Fossil Capital: From Water to Steam in the British Cotton Industry, *Historical Materialism*, 2013)

The need for access to resources has been a major cause of globalization throughout most of human history. This is particularly the case with natural resources that are location-dependent, like fossil fuels or ores and minerals, because access to them can become a problem when they are distributed unevenly across the world. For instance, the main reserves of oil and gas are in the Middle East, the main reserves of lithium (for batteries) are found in Australia, Chile and Bolivia, while Brazil holds more than ninety percent of the world reserves of niobium which is vital for nano-electrics. Other natural resources, like foodstuffs or timber, are not that location-dependent because they can be grown elsewhere, but even then some countries may have a monopoly position in the production of these goods, as is the case with wheat, cotton or coffee. Similar monopoly positions may also be attained in the production of high-tech technology, such as microchips and weapons.

Fossil reserves in the world (in 2024)

Known oil reserves (in billion barrels):		Known gas reserves (trillion m2)	
1. Venezuela	290	1. Russia	49
2. Saudi Arabia	270	2. Iran	29
3. Canada	170	3. Qatar	25
4. Iran	140	4. Turkmenistan	8
5. Iraq	120	5. Saudi Arabia	8
6. Kuwait	100	6. US	7
7. UAE	95	7. UAE	7
8. Russia	75	8. Venezuela	6
9. Libya	45	9. Nigeria	5
10. Kazakhstan	40	10. Algeria	4

To access resources and products that are not ubiquitous, the world has developed a dense global network of exploitation, production and transportation (which was the origin of the term 'globalization'). This globalization has also given rise to several global challenges, of which two will be discussed here: dependence on resources and environmental issues and climate change.

Coltan in Congo

Coltan is needed for smartphones, laptops and electric cars. Of the known reserves, 80 percent is in the Democratic Republic of Congo, located in the eastern part near Rwanda. However, the Congolese government has not been able to establish full authority over the exploitation and export of cobalt. This is mostly in the hands of the various rebel forces and Rwandese military that for years have been entangled in violent conflicts in the area.

Global challenge (1): dependence on resources

While the globalization of access, exploitation and distribution of resources may be considered beneficial to the world's well-being and economy, it has created dependencies. These dependencies are usually experienced on an individual level (who wants to give up their mobile phone, car, cotton shirt, coffee?) and consequently on a national level (the state will indulge these individual needs by facilitating production, trade, tariff reductions). But many of these dependencies have also become a challenge with global implications. One such challenge is the dependence of peoples and states on certain resources that are scarce or monopolized by a few. For instance, in 1973, when the Arab oil-producing states declared a boycott of oil export to some countries and raised the price of oil significantly, this caused a worldwide energy crisis. The dependency on oil from the Gulf region has also been one of (some argue: the main) cause of the 1991 Gulf War to evict Iraq from Kuwait. To meet this challenge of oil dependency, the United States started developing new technologies to extract oil from American soil by the controversial means of 'fracking', and in doing so have become independent from oil production elsewhere since the 2010s. China, on the other hand, which is in great need of a steady oil supply to sustain its growing economy, secured access to oil in several countries in the Gulf region, and exerts diplomatic pressure to maintain stability in that region to guarantee continued access to that oil (for example, China arranged a peaceful settlement between Iran and Saudi Arabia in 2023, two of the world's main oil producers). China also pursues a determined policy of obtaining and maintaining direct access to rare natural resources used for electronic devices and batteries.

Monopolizing rare earth elements

The demand for rare earth elements that are vital for electronics, renewable energy technology and weapon systems was 125,000 tons in 2021 and is expected to reach 315 tons in 2030. China does not possess these elements, but through investments in countries with such elements holds an estimated 60% of the world's exploitation of these elements, and 85% of the world's processing capacity.

(*BRINK News 7 August 2022, Brookings Institute 29 December 2022*)

Another global challenge is the dependency on global transport networks. This challenge became evident with the Covid-19 pandemic of 2019-2022. As a result of massive lockdowns, the transport networks were shut down as well. Consequently, people across the world were deprived of certain basic goods, including elementary components for medicines. It raised an awareness that it may not always be advantageous to specialize in the production of a limited number of goods, as certain economic doctrines prescribe, but that diversification of production may allow states to maintain a degree of economic self-reliance.

> **'Food miles'**
> With globalization and the constant demand for out-of-season produce, it is estimated that the average meal travels 2,500 kilometers before it lands on your plate.
> *(Foodwise, 'How Far Does Your Food Travel to Get to Your Plate?)*

> **Scarcity of fresh water**
> Almost 3/4 of the earth surface is water.
> Of this water only 1/20 (3.5 % of all water) is fresh water.
> Of this fresh water, 5/7 (2.5% of all water) is locked in the ice and ground,
> and only 2/7 (1% of all water) is directly available.
> Of this available fresh water, 3/4 is used for agriculture.

Global challenge (2): environmental issues and climate

Disputes over land, water or other resources are adressed at the negotiation table or in court, but also by hard power: a stronger country may build a dam in the river without having to care that the waterflow to the weaker neighboring country is being blocked; or it may send in the troops to occupy territory that is rich in minerals. This powerplay has been, and still is, part and parcel of human behavior in all three dimensions: local, national and global. In the 20th century, however, it gradually became clear that regional and international cooperation might be needed to address the accessibility and use of certain resources. This awareness targeted three concerns: the protection and depletion of, and pollution by resources.

> **International treaties on resources**
> - *The Antarctic Treaty* (1959): the continent of Antarctica shall not be subject to territorial claims, exploitation of resources, or ecological damaging.
> - *The Outer Space Treaty or Treaty on Principles Governing the Activities of States in the Exploration and Use of Outer Space, including the Moon and Other Celestial Bodies* (1966): no country can claim sovereignty or exclusive rights over celestial bodies or the moon which shall be used exclusively for peaceful purposes; their exploration is free to, and for the benefit and interests of all countries.
> - *United Nations Convention on the Law of the Sea* (1982): the deep see (beyond territorial waters) is free for peaceful and scientific exploration (as long as the acquired knowledge is made public afterwards); for mining and exploration, permission is required from the International Seabed Authority.

The **protection of environments** was the goal of international agreements on the protection of Antarctica, the deep sea and the moon. The aim of these agreements was to protect these environments against exploitation. Subsequent mostly national agreements aimed at protecting populations whose identity was closely connected to the land they inhabited. Safeguarding these environments was intended to ensure their survival, because in their belief system, removing them from their land would be tantamount to erasing their existence.

The 'personal' rights of natural resources

Natural resources like woods, rivers or mountains are commonly seen as inanimate objects that need protection from exploitation by means of international agreements. A new approach to such protection is to grant them the status as a **'legal personhood'** with its own rights. Often such rights are granted in recognition of claims of indigenous peoples to those places. Some examples of such legal personhoods are:

- the rainforest Te Urewera in New Zealand, as spiritual homeland of the Tūhoe people (2014).
- Whanganui River in New Zealand as part of the treaty settlement between the government and the Māori people (2017).
- Lake Erie in North America (2019): legal personhood granted by the city of Toledo (Ohio)
- Magpie River in Canada was granted nine rights, including the right to flow, the right to be safe from pollution – and the right to sue (2021).

The second concern relates to one of the effects of using resources: **pollution**. This is commonly dealt with bilaterally, like when states that share a river address pollution caused by factories upstream. It was carbon dioxide emissions, however, that generated awareness and concern globally. The cause of this pollution, it transpired, was largely human by excessive burning of fossil fuels and cattle farming. Scientists have unanimously come to the conclusion that this pollution is heating up the atmosphere which, in turn, is causing a **climate change**. These concerns have been voiced since the 1960s already but have only been treated by the international community as a global challenge since the 2010s. One of these challenges is the predicted large numbers of 'environmental refugees'.

A third concern that is on the mind of the international community is the **depletion of certain resources**. While one may consider this to be a global challenge, the international community has yet to address it as such. To date, the scramble for resources remains mostly a national and unilateral affair.

> **War or environment?**
>
> In 1992, 1,700 'concerned scientists' issued a warning that humanity had the choice to either spend its resources on war and violence, or on preventing catastrophic environmental damage. In 2017, the warning was reissued, this time signed by 15,000 scientists.
>
> *(Union of Concerned Scientists)*

Actors: the role of the consumer

The source of the environmental and resource dependency problems lies with states and (state) companies, but also with the individual consumer. The production and use of consumer goods make up a large portion of the resource depletion and environmental pollution. This means that the consumers can also play a role in the solution. Here we see friction between *ideas* and *interests*: even if one strongly believes that something needs to be done, how far is one willing to go in changing a lifestyle to meet the requirements of sustainable resource usage?

State, civil society and individual consumers are playing different but interconnected roles. Some individual consumers take the principled decision to change their lifestyle and hope, by doing so, that it may inspire others to follow suit. These actions may turn into social trends, or even into movements and NGOs that raise awareness but also pressure governments. Consumers, when united in action, have shown an ability to make quite a lobbying impact, often by boycotting certain products or producers.

The governments are the ones that can take measures that force an entire population to comply, by means of taxation, obligation or prohibition. These measures, however, may result in opposition from the population or from the professional groups that are most affected (like farmers, for instance, when confronted with measures to stop the use of pesticides or nitrogen emission from cattle). Since the 2010s, the resulting confrontation of interests and ideas have become major issues on the political agendas and the subject of court cases. It has caused both politicians and activists to complain about the decelerating mechanisms of democracy in times when decisive and quick action is needed.

Nexus

Addressing the misuse, lack, or scarcity of resources is a global challenge with multiple issues. Concerted actions to solve any of these issues yield several nexuses. In the case of misusing resources, the (simplified) example of the case of climate change may illustrate this. Addressing this global challenge is accomplished by focusing on its effects as well as its causes. Both generate several nexuses (see illustration). As regards the effects of climate change, one anticipates – and often already observes – rising sea waters, changing or disappearing agriculture, or freak weather events. These effects, in turn, may prompt people to migrate which then creates yet another nexus (and migration, as seen before, also has its own connections with security, economy, education, etc.). Addressing climate change, therefore, opens up a myriad of nexuses: the main culprit of climate change – carbon dioxide – is produced by cars (nexuses of transport, economy, leisure), by cattle (nexus of food production), by planes (nexuses of tourism, business), by industries (nexuses of economy, production of basic and consumer goods), by heating (nexuses of food production, personal well-being). Solutions are partly found in the requirement of people to abandon certain behavior (no meat, no cars, no planes), or by looking for alternatives (electric and nuclear power, meat substitutes).

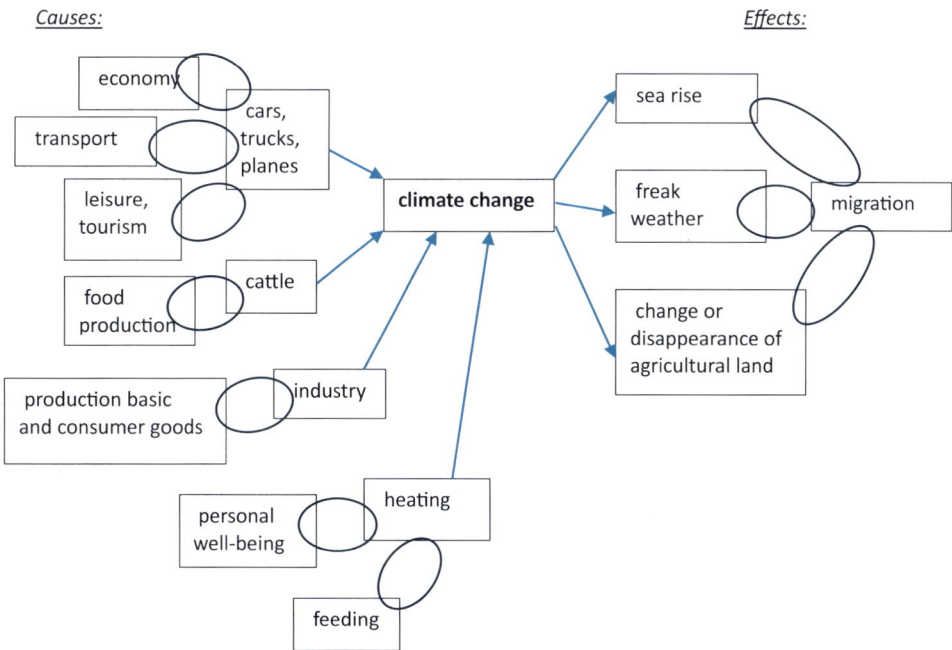

Figure IV.3.1 *Nexuses 'climate change'*

'Global' challenge?

While climate change and the (mis)use of resources are clearly affecting the world globally, it is less clear whether the concerted efforts needed to address this challenge should also be global. Many of the former colonized countries argue that it would be unfair that they should pay for the problems caused by their former colonizers. While this may be the case for carbon dioxide emissions, it is not necessarily the case for other types of pollution (like, for instance, plastic waste in the oceans - see text box).

Who is the polluter?

Carbon emission	Plastics in the ocean
1. China	1. China
2. United states	2. Indonesia
3. India	3. Philippines
4. Russia	4. Vietnam
5. Japan	5. Sri Lanka
6. Indonesia	6. Egypt
7. Iran	7. Thailand
8. Germany	8. Malaysia
9. South Korea	9. Nigeria
10. Saudi Arabia	10. Bangladesh

(https://www.worldometers.info/co2-emissions/co2-emissions-by-country/)
(https://www.statista.com/chart/12211/the-countries-polluting-the-oceans-the-most)

Another criticism that some former colonized countries level against the measures that are intended to stop climate change is that these measures will deny them the benefits from their upstarting economies while the Western countries have already reaped all those benefits. This is what has been referred to as the equity argument: rather than treating all countries equally (equal measures of carbon dioxide emission reduction, for instance), countries should be treated in accordance with their (in)capabilities. At the same time, for countries with less developed economies it is much easier to make the clean energy transition than it is for the developed economies. Some argue that this may even result in the less developed economies taking the lead in future developments.

Guyana's predicament

In 2015, vast reserves of oil were discovered in front of the coast of Guyana (South America). The income from the oil exploitation can be used for a much-needed development of the country. However, fossil fuels are also the cause for global heating and Guyana is one of the countries that is seriously threatened by rising sea levels.

Further reading

Edward B Barbier, 'Scarcity, frontiers and development,' *The Geographical Journal*, Vol.178, No.2, 2012, pp. 110-122

Carbon & Climate Law Review, Special Issue: Climate Change Politics In China: A Coming Of Age? Vol. 9, No. 3, 2015

Radoslav S. Dimitrov, 'Climate Diplomacy', in: Karin Bäckstrand, Eva Lövbrand (eds.), *Research Handbook on Climate Governance*, Edward Elgar Publishing, 2015

Charles Ogheneruonah Eghweree and Festus O. Imuetinyan, 'Africa and the Climate Change Diplomacy', *Journal of Sustainable Development*; Vol. 12, No. 2; 2019

Jeffrey A. Krautkraemer, 'Economics of Natural Resource Scarcity: The State of the Debate', *Resources for the Future*, April 2005 ● Discussion Paper

Oluwaseun J. Oguntuase, 'India and Africa Leverage Climate Diplomacy', *Observer Research Foundation: Issue Brief No.628*, 2023

CHAPTER 4

Security

People may feel insecure for a variety of reasons. Armed conflict is the most obvious reason, but since the 1990s we also see that terrorism, climate change and the absence of social well-being are sources of insecurity. This development has two implications for the world of today. First, the meaning of security has become much broader. Second, security has become a yardstick for many issues that the world faces: we speak of food security, energy security, migration security. It appears as though security addresses most of the basic human needs that until very recently were covered by human rights. This shift from human rights to security will be discussed in greater detail below.

That the term security has become so dominant gives the impression that people feel much more insecure than before. When one looks at the statistics of armed violence, however, this sense of insecurity is unjustified: armed violence may have increased in some forms (civil wars) but decreased in others (war between states, colonial war), and the total has been more or less the same since 1945. This prompts the conclusion that the sensation of (in)security is driven by other sources. One is the geopolitical positionality: insecurity may have increased among Europeans who after decades of peace are faced with a real or imagined threat from Russia, just like a sense of security may have increased among South Americans after decades of oppressive dictatorships had come to an end. Another source of increased insecurity is the multiplying factor of social media: today one has unlimited access to a non-stop stream of images and videos of war and violence on social media as opposed to the time when these images were distributed in limited quantity and frequency by the daily news outlets. Another factor is the sensation of insecurity itself. To feel insecure in the street is not restricted to warzones or places dominated by violent gangs; it also applies to a fear of crime or harassment, and even to the feeling of unease (e.g., because one is the only black man in an environment of white people, or because one is the only bare-headed woman in an environment of women with headscarves – or vice versa). Students reportedly at times feel insecure (or: 'unsafe') in a university when they are presented with information that they experience as offensive or too confrontational. It appears that security is not only to be free from fear of war, violence or starvation, but also to be free from feeling a threat to one's identity or sensitivities.

In this chapter we will discuss how (in)security has become a global challenge and how, in addressing this challenge, there has been an increase in the focus on security.

Terrorism

One of today's main global security concerns is terrorism. Terrorism still lacks a clear definition but is usually described as the killing of political leaders or random people with the purpose of disrupting a governmental or political system. But many organizations also use terrorist means for other goals, like the proclaimed liberation of their people or country from oppression or foreign occupation (examples are the IRA in Ireland, ANC in South Africa, PLO and Hamas in Israel, Tamil Tigers in Sri Lanka). In many of these instances, terrorism is not a *goal*, but a *means*: this distinction is important for reasons that will be discussed below.

Terrorism has a long history but was first addressed as a global phenomenon during the 1970s, when several so-called left-extremist organizations were actively aiming to destabilize the county (like 'Lightning Path' in Peru, JAL in Japan, RAF in Germany, Brigade Rosso in Italy). Terrorism became recognized as a global *challenge* in the early 2000s with the 'War on Terror', which focused primarily on the emerging Islamic militantism around the world. This War on Terror was declared by the United States after they had suffered several simultaneous attacks on 11 September 2001, and it prompted a world-wide effort to combat terrorism.

Combatting terrorism usually aims at preventing the attack rather than prosecuting the attackers afterwards (which is the common action taken in any criminal prosecution). To prevent terrorism, state security apparatuses are trying to predict and anticipate terrorist activities. Since the early 2000s, states are also cooperating more than before in exchanging intelligence. As a result, a veritable global counter terrorism industry has emerged with its own information networks. One side effect (or: nexus) of this is the ways in which the counter terrorism may violate the principles of the rule of law. For instance, how far is one willing to go in the interrogation of a terrorist suspect if that may prevent other terrorist attacks? And is one willing to expand the legally limited time for incarceration of a suspect if there is still no sufficient evidence against the terrorist suspect? Another nexus is the way the counter-terrorism measures affect the privacy of the public. People can be monitored and tracked by cameras in the streets and buildings, by means of their mobile devices, money transfers, travel itineraries. Consequently, balancing the public interest of security and the individual interest of privacy has become a challenge within the larger challenge of global terrorism.

Another way of preventing terrorism is to focus on its **root causes**. This appears to be quite complex. In terms of the 3-I's, the discussion revolves around the question of whether the causes are rooted in *interests, ideas or identities*. Do people rebel violently (including through terrorist activities) because they are poor, or because they resent oppression, or because they want to liberate their country? If these interests are indeed the root cause, then it is also clear that the terrorism will end once these interests are addressed. To some observers, however, *ideas* rather than *interests* are the main drivers for many terrorist groups. According to these observers, communism, anarchism, or Islamism are belief systems that promote or endorse violence as part of their ideology. Other observers hold that these ideologies are not causes of terrorism but provide the discourse that justifies their actions. From this perspective, countering terrorism means that one needs to counter the ideology (in intelligence terms: to provide a 'counternarrative'). A recent development in terrorist activities is that they appear to be prompted by issues of identity. The terrorist killings by white supremacists are the clearest example, but one might also include the communities who feel that their very existence is under threat and that they are fighting for their survival (examples are the Palestinians in the Occupied Palestinian Territories, Tamils in Sri Lanka, Kurds in eastern Turkey). In all cases, however, there is a combination of factors at play that may explain the use of terrorist means.

Peacemaking, building and keeping

Universities today offer courses in Conflict Studies, Terrorism Studies and Security Studies, but hardly ever in Peace Studies. While peace may be defined as the absence of conflict, the processes of peacemaking and peace building require entirely different analyses and actions than ending conflicts. While peacemaking is the action of deciding what conditions are to be met to end hostile relations, peacebuilding is the elaborate process before and afterwards that focuses on trust and social interactions. Peacekeeping, on the other hand, is a term that is usually reserved for a military presence by a third party in a conflict with the aim to prevent further violence.

'Peace' is more than the absence of war, however. Given the widening of domains where insecurity is experienced, it is argued that an equal widening of the notion of peace is needed. Here, the concept of **polarization** is important: the hostile opposition between two or more factions represented by political, ethnic, religious or regional groups (see also the notion of 'multipolarization' elsewhere in this textbook). The manifestation of such hostile opposition has grown to include discrimination, hate speech, vengefulness and even violence and conflict, both within states and among states. From that perspective, the notion of peace is not only relevant on the global level, but also on the national and local: schools, neighborhoods, cities and societies anywhere in the world (and perhaps mostly so in the West) experience the challenges of such types of polarization.

Peace is a notion that is commonly related to states. The United Nations charter states that it wants to 'maintain peace and security' among states and peoples, but it fails to set any guidelines on how to achieve that. The United Nations mostly started out as a mediator of conflicts, but it gradually grew in a role of preventing international conflicts. While mediation is a typical form of soft power, prevention can also be a form of hard power: the United Nations started to act as the policeman of the world by sending peacekeeping forces to places where conflicts could erupt or after – and that was usually the case– a conflict had erupted, and where peacekeepers were stationed to keep the warring parties separated. These peacekeepers consisted of army units that various states committed to the peacekeeping force of that conflict. This marked an interesting change in many armies, especially in those of smaller states: the national military did not only serve the defence of one's own country, it could also serve the peace processes in countries around the world. Countries who commit their military to a peacekeeping force may do so to contribute to world peace. But more often do they do so to show their goodwill to the world community which, in turn, might pay off in the future when favors are required.

The main problem in peacekeeping is the issue of sovereignty. It is one thing to place a peacekeeping force on the borders between two warring states with the permission of those two states. But it's quite a different thing when a conflict is happening within a country, like a civil war, a massacre, a genocide. What if the government refuses any foreign interference? And what if that government is the main perpetrator of the violence? State sovereignty is generally sacrosanct: no interference is allowed in domestic affairs without the permission of the government. This principle started to waver after the 1994 genocide in Rwanda.

Genocide in Rwanda (1994)

The Hutu majority government of Rwanda had incited violence against the Tutsi population, and within a matter of days between half a million and a million Tutsis were massacred, mostly with machetes. The world watched in horror, but no country intervened. A United Nations peace keeping mission was already present, but they were not allowed to interfere because their UN-mandate was to oversee the implementation of a peace accord between Rwanda and its neighbour Uganda. When the United Nations finally obtained a Security Council declaration which gave the mandate to intervene in the ongoing genocide, it was already too late.

'Responsibility to Protect' (R2P)

When considering the principle of state sovereignty in the case of internal conflicts within a state, like civil war or genocide, it may be useful to draw a comparison with the situation of a burning house, or with domestic violence. Do we wait for the fire department or the police to arrive, or should we rush in to help and prevent worse? In 1999, some members of the international community decided on the latter during the Yugoslavian civil war. When Kosovo declared independence from Serbia (then still officially called Yugoslavia), atrocities committed by Serbian forces against Kosovan civilians shocked European powers, who still had the 1995 images of the massacres committed by Serbian forces against Bosnian Muslims fresh in their minds, and the genocide in Rwanda a year before that. Was the world to stand by and watch another massacre? A resolution to act before the United Nations was blocked by Russia. But NATO, the American-European military alliance, argued that they had a 'Responsibility to Protect', and bombarded Serbian forces and strategic targets within Serbia. And again in 2011, NATO invoked this principle to bombard the military forces of Khaddafi who were about to violently suppress the 'Arab Spring' revolt in Libya.

Until that point, the United Nations had kept quiet. After all, the sanctity of state sovereignty is one of its foundations. But many (not all!) members of the international community agreed that intervention was sometimes needed to prevent human catastrophes from taking place. This required a rethink of the notion of sovereignty. It was considered politically too sensitive to make the Responsibility to Protect an *exception* to sovereignty. A more elegant solution was *expanding* the notion of sovereignty. It was argued that sovereignty implies a **dual responsibility:** externally, to respect the sovereignty of other states, but also internally, to respect the dignity and basic rights of all the people within the state. It is important to realize that this is not a rule of law set in stone, it is still under discussion, and for many states it is controversial.

Human security

The discussions about possible exceptions to the sanctity of the principle of sovereignty were prompted by considerations regarding citizens of a state rather than the state itself. This meant that the conversations about the relation between the international and national also permeated to the third level of the 3-D-chessboard: to the local and the individual. Before, these levels were usually discussed in different frameworks: states were viewed in terms of security, people in terms of human rights. By the 1990s, these two concepts converged in the notion of 'human security'.

The first official mention of human security was in the *Human Development Report* of 1994. It was introduced because the existing terminology was considered inadequate: 'security' was still too much seen in terms of state security, and in humanitarian law, where not states but people were placed under protection of international law, security was still only seen in terms of armed conflicts. Now, in 1994, the concept of security was to include chronic threats such as disease, hunger, unemployment, political repression. This was termed human security. However, at the time, this notion was not framed in terms of security, nor in terms of law, but in terms of development.

Ever since its introduction, the concept of human security has been evolving. At first, human security was seen in material terms, meaning the struggle against poverty and disease and hunger. Later, human security was extended to include values and identity. Nowadays, the term human security has become common usage both in the academic world and in the world of development policy.

Human security

There is general consensus among policymakers and academics that human security has four key characteristics:
1. Human security may be discussed in material terms, like food, or energy, or migration, but it is about the people.
2. Human security is a global concern because it is of importance to any individual wherever they may be.
3. The consequences of insecurity can travel beyond borders.
4. Early prevention rather than later intervention is the best way to go about ensuring human security.

A question is how the notion of human security relates to human development. Some see a clear distinction between the two: human development has to do with choices, and therefore with empowerment (also described as the security *of* basic human needs), while human security has to do with protection *from* unwanted situations. But for others, the two are interrelated or even the same. This argument was made by a group of intellectuals from all over the world and included Amartya Sen, who in 2003 produced a report with the telling title *Human Security Now*. They defined human security as the protection of the vital core of all human lives in ways that enhance human freedoms and human fulfilment. Human security is a dynamic concept, the report says, because its meaning varies across individuals and societies. Because of that dynamic nature, the report deliberately does offer an itemized list of what makes up human security: that needs to be decided separately in every situation. Based on these discussions, the concept of human security has been criticized for being too vague and therefore ineffective as a useful tool of analysis in policymaking.

'Securitization'

Security has become the new nexus in many global issues that have, since the turn of the millennium, been framed in security terms: economy, pandemic, migration, development. According to some observers, this is the result of an increased 'securitization' of these issues. This specific term describes how an issue is presented as being under such a threat that immediate action must be undertaken. Securitization comprises three elements. First, there is an *existential threat*, that is a threat to the very existence of a community. This threat can be physical – being bombed or wiped out in a genocide – but also existential, that is, a threat to the preservation of a culture and identity. Here, security is about survival. The second element is that this threat is so imminent that there is no time to waste, that *immediate action* is required. We can imagine this to be the case when an army marches across the border, but similar images are used with immigrants crossing borders. The third element is the need for *decisive action*, preferably by a strong leader who will not compromise but who will do what it takes to get the job done to safeguard the security of the nation, even if it demands exceptional measures.

The Copenhagen School on 'Securitization Theory'
Securitization is a successful speech act 'through which an intersubjective understanding is constructed within a political community to treat something as an existential threat to a valued referent object, and to enable a call for urgent and exceptional measures to deal with the threat'.
(Barry Buzan, Ole Wæver and Jaap de Wilde, *Security: A New Framework of Analysis*, 1998)

Securitization can be legitimate, but the Securitization Theory was developed to describe situations where securitization is an abuse of power for political and populist purposes. For example, the Covid-19 pandemic was a health issue that in 2019 became securitized: it was considered an existential threat because it could kill people extensively and therefore demanded immediate action. In democracies one witnessed leaders setting aside regular democratic processes so they could take decisive action that they claimed to be justified as a safeguard of the nation's security. Many considered this a legitimate securitization, while some claimed that it was an unfounded abuse of power.

Academics observe an increase of securitization as an abuse of power for political and populist purposes. They criticize the ease with which issues are being securitized. Part of that criticism is directed at the exaggerated urgency that is evoked by security language. For example, military metaphors like 'war on drugs', 'war on terror', or 'war on crime' are being used to emphasize – some will say: exaggerate – the urgency of these issues. This type of language evokes the image of imminent threats to society which demand exceptional measures. Other critics point out that when an issue is treated in terms of security, there is a tendency to lose sight of other aspects. This has happened with religion (the focus on Islamically justified terrorism has made religion in general suspect), terrorism (that label prevents one from considering the motives of freedom fighters who use terrorist means), and migration (migrants are perceived as an economic or cultural threat rather than as a people in need or as a solution to economic and demographic decline).

Further reading

Alex J. Bellamy. 'The responsibility to protect – five years on', *Ethics & International Affairs*, Vol. 24, No. 2 (2010), pp. 143–169

Commission on Human Security, *Human Security Now*, New York, UNHCR, 2003,

European Union Institute for Security Studies, *Contestation. The new dynamic driving global politics*, 2024

International Commission on Intervention and State Sovereignty, *The Responsibility to Protect*, December 2001

Oliver Jütersonke & Keith Krause, 'Peace, Security and Development in Post-Conflict Environments,' *Security Dialogue*, Vol. 36, No. 4 (2005)

Inge Kaul, Mahlub ul Haq, et al., *Human Development Report of 1994*, United Nations Development Programme (UNDP), Oxford University Press, 1994

Holger Stritzel, 'Towards a Theory of Securitization: Copenhagen and Beyond', *European Journal of International Relations*, Vol. 13, No.3 (2007). pp. 357–383

CHAPTER 5

Unwanted migration

Since the 1990s it is mostly the United States and Europe that have put migration at the top of the list of their political problems. However, many other countries across the world are also dealing with large numbers of migrants. As discussed in the chapter on migration as a global structure, 'migrants' is a generic term for people who are moving from one country to other countries ('international migration') or within in their own country ('domestic migration'), either voluntarily or forced, whereby the causes for migration can differ considerably. Migration may become a challenge when one of two issues come into play: the migration is unwanted in the destination country (this is the issue of illegal or undocumented migration) or when there is a sudden and significant movement of migrants (this is the case with displaced persons or refugees). The question, however, is when such a challenge can be considered a global challenge.

Global challenge – who?

International migrants pose a problem when they are unwanted. This is in stark contrast to the migrants who have been invited. For instance, countries like Canada, Australia and the United States have migration policies that regulate migration, primarily by identifying the types of professions that their societies need. Member states of the European Union have opened their borders to each other with the deliberate purpose of having unhindered exchange of 'goods and people'. Israel welcomes immigration of all Jewish people. In all these instances, migration is wanted, albeit for a variety of motives, and subject to strict regulations.

Migrants can be unwanted for several reasons. **'Illegal' (or: 'undocumented')** **migrants** are migrants who enter a country regardless of the migration rules of that country. This type of migration is mostly of an economic nature: people are seeking a better life. This is what international migration organizations call 'voluntary migration' (although we have seen that the voluntary nature of such migration can be disputed). These two types of migration are usually undertaken by individuals: people decide for themselves if and when they want to migrate.

The other types of international migration that may pose a problem are the **displaced persons (or: refugees)** who are fleeing war, famine or political oppression. A difference with the 'undocumented' migrants is that refugees usually move in large groups at the same time following a sudden disastrous event. This is also known as 'forced migration', which may be relatively small on the world scale in 2024 estimated to be (1.4 percent of the total world population) but can be very substantial for countries who are receiving these migrants. Another important difference is that only refugees who are recognized as such hold **legal status**. Under the international Refugee Convention, these refugees are entitled to settlement in other countries, either as individuals who apply for asylum in another country, or under the auspices of the International Organization of Migration (IOM) and the United Nations High Commission of Refugees (UNHCR), which will finance and create shelters for large communities of refugees.

A new pressing reason of migration is **climate change**. Rising sea levels, temperature changes and droughts are causing people to move away from their homes. While reference to these people is usually made with the descriptive term 'climate migrants', the legal term 'climate refugees' is also being applied: while the first term is descriptive, the second term implies certain rights of protection under the Refugee Convention.

UNHCR: climate refugees

"In the last decade, the interlinkages between climate change impacts and conflict have become particularly apparent. In 2022, 70 per cent of refugees and asylum seekers fled from highly climate-vulnerable countries, an increase from 56 per cent in 2012.8 Climate change and environmental degradation increasingly drive displacement, in combination with social, economic and political factors. Many countries are affected by both conflict and disaster that interact and overlap as triggers and drivers of displacement."

(UNHCR, *Focus Area Strategic Plan for Climate Action 2024-2030*)

Global challenge - where?

A 'global' challenge implies that an event has global repercussions. However, the situation of illegal and forced migration mostly involves two or several countries (one country of origin and one or more neighboring countries of destination). Strictly speaking, problems posed in these situations present challenges to both the originating and arriving countries. The question then is: when does migration become a global challenge? In other words, in what instances does migration affect people worldwide, and needs to be addressed through the concerted efforts of various actors?

Displaced persons or refugees

In the case of displaced persons and refugees, their migration is often very localized (mostly domestic or crossing only one border). It may nevertheless be considered a global challenge because of its frequency and because it happens worldwide. Moreover, a war or a drought that causes a sudden and massive displacement of people anywhere in the world necessitates immediate and large-scale humanitarian aid. These considerations have prompted the international community to establish international organizations like the IOM and the UNHCR to manage such situations. They are equipped with the means and finances to act swiftly and practically. In most instances of a refugee crisis, they will create large camps to shelter the refugees and provide them with food and medical care.

Refugees: countries of origin and destination (2024)

Countries that host the most refugees:
1. Iran (3.8 million)
2. Turkey (3.3 million)
3. Pakistan (3.0-4.0 million)
4. Colombia (2.9 million)
5. Germany (2.6 million)

Countries from where most refugees originate:
1. Afghanistan (6.4 million)
2. Syrian Arab Republic (6.4 million)
3. Venezuela (6.1 million)
4. Ukraine (5 million)
5. South Sudan (2.3 million)

(https://www.unhcr.org/refugee-statistics)

Illegal or undocumented migrants

Illegal migration can acquire a large regional dimension in case of **lengthy trajectories of international migration**. Europe and the United States are two examples, with undocumented migrants trying to reach Europe from Africa and Asia, and the United States from Central and South America. Here, not only the countries of origin and arrival are affected, but also the countries of transit that lie between. For instance, for decades there has been an increasing flow of illegal migrants from Central and South American countries heading for the United States.

While Mexico serves as both a country of transit and origin, many migrants do not make it across the American-Mexican border, and they remain stuck in Mexico, which therefore becomes the involuntary destination country, thereby creating its own set of problems. A different example of long-distance illegal migration is the one heading for Europe. While the United States is a single-country of destination, the European Union is a multi-country destination with multiple-entry possibilities. If each European country were to take its own measures to regulate or even stop the migration, the problem is not solved but repositioned to the next country. Such unilateral actions can create a waterbed effect: if one pushes on one side, it will rise on the other side. Concerted efforts among the countries of destination will therefore be needed to address this migration issue.

Global challenge - what?

If unwanted 'migrants' of any type (undocumented, refugees, or any other) are said to pose a global challenge, what exactly, then, is that challenge? While these discussions tend to focus on the countries of destination, there are also challenges for the **countries of origin**. For instance, the departure of large segments of the population may leave agricultural land untilled or a society without skilled workers. This may, in turn, generate more migration, leading to a vicious cycle. Psychological and social problems of the migrants themselves pose another challenge: large numbers of displaced persons and refugees, in particular, often face lengthy periods of time when they live in remote places in basic conditions waiting to return to their homeland. While this may be deplorable on humanitarian grounds, it may also give rise to other concerns: the concentrations of large numbers of displaced persons may be disruptive to their psychological wellbeing, and may even cause some among them to be so disgruntled and resentful that there is a possibility that they become a security risk (as was one of the causes of the rise of the Taliban).

The rise of the Taliban

The 1979 invasion of the Soviet Union in Afghanistan and the ensuing civil war caused the first large waves of Afghan refugees to Iran and Pakistan. In Pakistan, the refugee camps housed an estimated 4 million Afghan refugees. In these camps, Islamic schools (*madrassas*) provided basic education, but also gave rise to the Taliban ('students') who after 1994 became a prominent force in the civil war. They established an 'Islamic emirate' in large part of Afghanistan from 1996 to 2001, were thereafter subdued by American-led allied forces, but resurged in 2021 when they took power in entire Afghanistan.

Most discussions about migration as a global challenge focus on the **countries of destination**. The main problem is said to be the number of 'migrants', although it is not always clear to whom this generic term refers. Most often it refers to refugees and illegal migrants, but in the public and political discourse of many Western countries this category of migrants is mixed up with residents of these countries who are of migrant origin from non-Western countries. As a result, the discussions of the nature of the migration as a global (or national) challenge are quite diffuse, ranging from the impact of migration on the demographics, economy and society of the country of origin or destination. These will be discussed in the following paragraphs.

> "Mass migrations are inevitable, and more than ever, they are necessary. (...) The world of tomorrow is not only full of mobile people but is defined by the mobility of everything."
> (Parag Khanna, *Move. How Mass Migration will Reshape the World*, 2022)

Impact on demographics

A large influx of people can disrupt the demographics of the country of destination. However, the notion of a demographic disruption is relative, and mostly related to the nature of influx and the type of migrants.

In the case of **displaced persons and refugees**, the influx of migrants is usually sudden and substantial. However, the aim of these migrants is not to stay, but to return to their country of origin. Their stay is therefore intended as temporary, although reality may be different. The approximately 700 thousand Palestinians who fled their country in 1948 were given shelter in neighboring countries like Syria, Lebanon and Jordan with the expectation to return, but they still have not. Similarly, millions of refugees from Afghanistan have for decades been living in neighboring countries Pakistan and Iran with the hope of return. In such cases, the original temporary refugee camps have gradually been reshaped into towns and suburbs.

> **Largest refugee camps in 2024**
> Kutupalung (Bangladesh): 930,000 refugees (from Myanmar)
> Kakuma (north Kenya): 200,000 refugees (from Sudan)
> Dadaab (south Kenya): 240,000 refugees (from Somalia)
> Za'tari (Jordan): 100,000 (from Syria)

In some instances, refugees have been granted asylum in countries further away. And although they may still aim to return to their home country, many create a new life in their destination country. This seems also to be the case with most of the (legal as well as illegal) labor migrants: they might intend to migrate for temporary work only, but many stay on and build their lives in the destination country and try to acquire legal residence.

If significant numbers of both wanted and unwanted migrants remain in the destination country, this will have an impact on the demographics of that country. In some countries, migration can be a **restorative demographic** factor. In countries where the population is declining, there will be fewer young people to sustain the economy and care for the growing number of elderly people. Migration can restore this balance. On the other hand, migration can also be seen as disruptive to a country's demographics if the migrants are of a **different ethnicity or religion** than the people of that country. This is the case when the self-proclaimed 'original' population fears for a 'dilution' of its characteristic features by people of different color, race, culture or religion (see elaboration below, under 'Impact on society').

Migrant health care workers after Brexit

One of the motivating factors behind the United Kingdom leaving the European Union in 2021 ('Brexit') was to put a stop to migration. However, Brexit also put a stop to intra-European migration. As a result, the health care system lost many of its workers from EU countries. To compensate for this loss of work force, large numbers of health care workers have been recruited from India, Nigeria and Zimbabwe.

(Center for Global Development, *Blog post 19 February 2024*)

Impact on economy

A large influx of people can disrupt a country's economy. This is the case when the influx is sudden and substantial, as in the case of displaced persons and refugees. While in most of these cases the refugees are housed by international organizations, there will always be a spillover into urban areas, resulting in rising rents for houses and apartments, falling salaries, and the shortages and overpricing of food, medicine and daily necessities. An example is the more than one million Syrian refugees in the small country of Lebanon with a population of five million. This was caused by the Syrian civil war in 2014 but was exacerbated by the Israeli attacks in 2024 that caused half a million Lebanese to flee their homes and seek shelter elsewhere in the country. Such disruptions are not usually the case in Western countries, although this economic argument is often used in the political discussions about migration.

Impact on society

The complaints about migration are mostly heard in Western countries, and while the arguments against migration are often couched in terms of demographic and economic disruption, the concerns are usually cultural. These concerns are directed at migrants who are ethnically and culturally different from the residents of the destination country. The arrival of large numbers of such migrants can be seen as disruptive to the cultural structures and social cohesion of that society (although there is always the question of what is the tipping point is of these 'large' numbers: when do they become disruptive to the local culture?). In this way, the discussion of migration shifts from concerns about *interests* ('they take our jobs') to concerns about *identity* ('I cannot be myself anymore') or even insecurity ('I feel unsafe in my own country').

These cultural concerns play no or a lesser role in countries where migrants share the ethnic or cultural identity of the residents of that country. This may explain the welcome of the 6 million Ukrainian refugees in Europe in 2022 as opposed to the 1 million Syrian refugees in 2017. This may also explain why the discussions about cultural concerns are more likely to be heard in Europe and the United States than in countries like Iran or Pakistan, where the millions of mostly Afghan refugees mostly share the culture and language of those countries. One may wonder if the reception of these Afghan refugees would have been different if they had been Ukrainian. Could this, then, be the reason why **racism** or **xenophobia** is more present in these discussions in Western countries, or are these sentiments innate to the Western mindset, as has been argued?

This situation may also explain why discussions about migration in Western countries are often about **identity** and **values**. Obviously, these societies feel that their own cultural identity and value system is threatened by migrants from different backgrounds. Whether this concern is justified is not easily answered, but it clearly plays an important role in the political debates in these societies. What is relevant for the student of International Studies, however, is to realize that these debates encompass the local and national to the global level: they have permeated political and academic debates about global spheres identified on the basis of culture (and often religion), which are in turn assumed by some to be 'clashing' because of the nature of their cultural and religious differences.

> **Nativism** is the term used for the position that the interests and culture of the native citizens should be protected against those of the citizens of migrant origin. Problematic in nativist thought is that the 'native' does not include the indigenous people in countries like America or Australia, nor migrants of colour who have lived there for generations.

Nexuses

When migration is considered a global challenge, then there are numerous nexuses to consider when trying to make a concerted effort to address this challenge. For example, if migration is considered a challenge for a particular destination, that region may seek to physically stop the influx of migrants, but it may also seek to address the causes of migration. These causes can be diverse: civil war, lack of economic prospects, political persecution, natural disasters. Addressing each of these causes will, in turn, open a series of nexuses (see figure IV.5.1). For example, if the cause of migration is identified as a lack of economic prospects (see figure IV.5.1), then creating such prospects may involve the improving education, civil society, and good governance. And if the focus is on education, for example, experience has shown that educating girls contributes considerably to improving a country's economy – another nexus of women's empowerment.

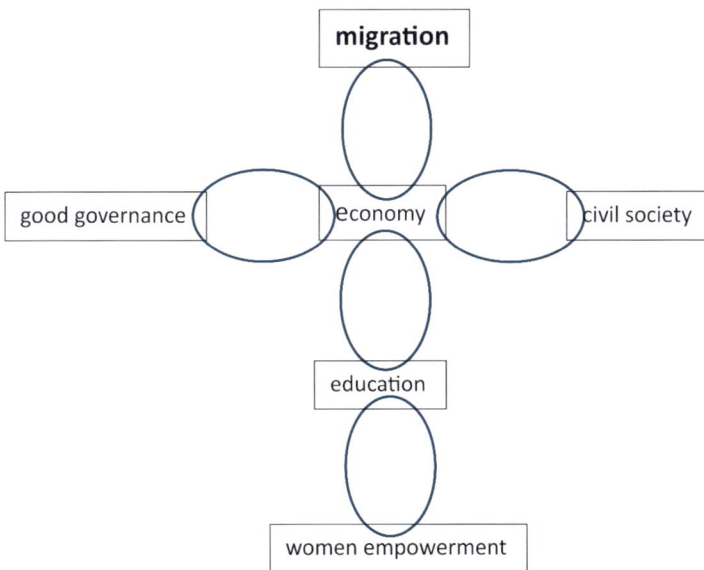

Figure IV.5.1 Nexus migration - economy

If, on the other hand, the country or region of destination decides to physically stop migration, migration becomes a security issue, and another set of nexuses emerges (see figure IV.5.2). One is the strengthening of borders through walls, gates, and border patrols, which is the nexus of policing. Another nexus is cooperation with neighboring countries, where deals can be made, for example, that this neighboring country will host all migrants in exchange for financial (or other) compensation. This may lead to a different set of issues, for instance that this neighboring country now has political leverage over the country that wants to stop immigration ('we will let the migrants through unless you meet our demands'), or that a large presence of migrants could destabilize this neighboring country (which is a threat to the country that wants to stop migration), or that these migrants could become the recruitment ground for criminal or terrorist organizations (as was the case with the Taliban, who were recruited among the Afghan refugee communities in Pakistan). When these issues are addressed, they become new nexuses.

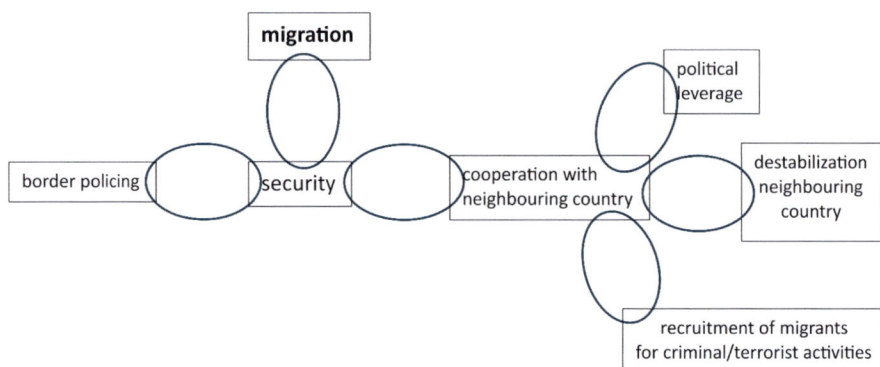

Figure IV.5.2 *Nexus migration - security*

Further reading

Global Governance, Special: International Migration, Vol. 16, No. 3, 2010

Hein de Haas, *How Migration Really Works: The Facts About the Most Divisive Issue in Politics*, Basic Books, 2023

IOM, annual reports

Rahel Kunz, Sandra Lavenex, Marion Panizzon (eds.), *Multilayered Migration Governance. The Promise of Partnership*, Routledge, 2011

UNHCR, *Focus Area Strategic Plan for Climate Action 2024-2030*,

World Economic Forum, *Climate refugees - the world's forgotten victims*, 2021

CHAPTER 6

Pandemics and global health

Epidemics – unexpected or seasonal outbreaks of a disease in in a community or geographically confined population – are a regular occurrence in history. Epidemics do not have to be infectious: for instance, obesity is considered an epidemic in America. An epidemic becomes a pandemic when the disease is infectious, and spreads exponentially across borders. Influenza, for instance, is an annually recurring sickness in Europe, the two Americas and southeast Asia, causing an estimated 300-600 thousand deaths per year. Pandemics cause most concern when they have a high death rate. In the 6th and 14th century, the plague devastated societies in Europe, Asia and North Africa, and in the 16-17th century, smallpox did the same to the indigenous populations of the two Americas. Similarly, cholera outbreaks were regular occurrences in unhygienic and densely populated areas across the world, and the Spanish Flu of 1918 caused an estimated 50-100 million deaths worldwide. Certain serious infectious diseases like polio or yellow fever have been mostly eradicated by means of vaccinations or are confined ('endemic') to certain regions. Malaria is also an endemic disease because the mosquitos that transmit the disease only live to certain areas in the world.

Until recently, pandemics seemed less threatening, either because there were vaccinations against them or because they were relatively quickly contained. The Covid-19 pandemic of 2019-2022 shattered that complacency: it wreaked world-wide havoc with an estimated 7 million deaths and caused massive lockdowns and other restrictive measures. However, Covid-19 should not have come as such a surprise because it had been preceded by a succession of similar pandemics caused by virus transmission between wildlife and humans: in 2003, Sars erupted in in China and spread to 26 countries in four months; in 2005, the Asian flu spread around the world; in 2009, the Swine flu (also known as the Mexican flu) spread to 30 countries within weeks; and in 2014, Ebola broke out in West Africa (but it was quickly contained), killing 1 out of every 3 patients.

While all these pandemics caused global challenges, not all were considered or treated as such. That was different with the Covid-19 pandemic: global concerted efforts went into containing the disease. However, critics have argued that the international response was only deemed necessary once the pandemic affected Western countries. While that may be the case, pandemics like Sars, Swine flu and Ebola, which took place in the decades before that, had been contained with far fewer victims than Covid-19, which might have been the reason for the initial false optimism that Covid-19 could also be quickly contained.

Global action

A global challenge requires an international concerted action to meet the global crisis at hand. Already in 1851, it was suggested that international coordination was required to fight pandemics like cholera, but it wasn't until the United Nations was founded before such a coordinating body came to life. It was mainly on the insistence of non-Western member states that the World Health Organization (WHO) was founded in 1948. All UN states were automatically member of this organization and each country had an equal vote. The goal of the WHO was to improve public health worldwide.

The function of the WHO was not entirely clear at first. Was the WHO to act only in response to crises, or was it to act in a preventive capacity? The first option was subject to much political controversy among the member states, mainly because some member states were unwilling to give up part of their sovereignty in health policies. Preventive action in specific cases, on the other hand, was considered less controversial and in the 1960s the WHO took on the job of eliminating smallpox. This was a very contagious disease that was also deadly: about 3 out of every 10 patients died. Many smallpox survivors have permanent scars over large areas of their body, especially their faces, and some survivors were left blind. The fight against smallpox took place at the height of the Cold War but was one of the few international operations in which the United States and Soviet Union worked together. By 1979, the WHO officially declared smallpox eradicated.

From the 1970s onwards, the WHO started taking on the role of coordinator of global public health rather than only combatting existing or emerging world diseases. The reason for this change was the great addition of new states that had achieved independence as former colonies and had become automatic members of the WHO through their membership of the United Nations. Most of these countries had serious national health issues and were in need of a powerful and active international body to address these problems. This pressure on its role as coordinator was effective because in 1978, the WHO declared health a fundamental **human right** and, consequently, every government was to be responsible for granting its population easy access to health care.

The case of Covid-19

The 3-I's – interests, ideas, identity – provide a useful framework for analyzing the way the world handled the Covid-19 pandemic.

While international solidarity and coordination would have been the most adequate means to fight the pandemic, national *interests* quickly took over. Every state wanted to take care of itself. When Spain and Italy were the first to be hit by the pandemic in Europe in 2020, they asked for extra European financial assistance. This was initially refused with the argument that they only had themselves to blame for their financial distress because of the economic mess they had allowed to persist for years. Especially the fact that Italy was a member of the G7, the group of the seven wealthiest countries in the world, was a point of contention: some EU countries that were not G7 members wondered why they should pay for Italy. While these arguments may make sense from an economic perspective, they certainly lacked in compassion and solidarity in a public health crisis. A similar lack of solidarity arose once a vaccine for Covid-19 was developed: Western countries hoarded these vaccines and were already offering their populations their second or third round of inoculations when people in African countries were still waiting for their first.

Fighting the pandemic also meant states had to prioritize their interests. Did public health trump economic interests? Did public health justify a government intruding on people's lives with requirements for medical checkups, obligatory health insurances, vaccination programs? Was public health so important that it justified school children and students missing months of education and years of social interaction? Although it was predicted that the shutdown of international trade and national economies would lead to a worldwide economic collapse once the pandemic was over, this did not happen. On the other hand, the impact of the lockdowns on the social and psychological wellbeing of people appears to be greater and longer lasting than anticipated.

In several instances, the policy decisions taken by countries hit by the pandemic were not based on interests, but on *ideas*, and mostly beliefs. Some government leaders flatly refused to acknowledge that there was a pandemic at all, or that Covid-19 was much different from any other type of influenza. This kind of attitude wasn't restricted to governments. In quite a few – mostly Western – countries, conspiracy theories arose about governments using the lockdowns and vaccination programs to control the people. An important dimension of beliefs pertained to the notion of freedom, which became an important topic of discussion especially in Western countries. The central issue of the debate was whether people should have the freedom to refuse vaccination or that such refusal would lead to the violation of the right of others to be free of disease and the threat of contamination.

Internationally, *identity* showed up when the pandemic gave rise to a blame game with Africans calling Covid-19 the 'white plague' because they blamed the

Europeans for transmitting it, and Europeans calling it the Chinese disease because it had started in that country. This 'us versus them' was not conducive to the much-needed international solidarity and coordination. Other identity issues played out on the national level, often illustrating cultural differences among people. In some countries people were better at observing the strict lockdown imposed by their governments, while in other countries people revolted against the police and their government. Lockdowns also prompted very different responses from people that can perhaps be explained in terms of cultural identity. An illustrative, albeit stereotypical example is that in the United States there were long lines of people queuing at gun stores in the hours before a lockdown, while in the Netherlands there were long lines at the marihuana shops. The use of face masks also showed interesting cultural differences: in China and most Southeast Asian countries, face masks were used to prevent the spread of germs *to* other people, while in mostly Western countries, face masks were used to be protected *against* the germs of other people.

International mechanisms

When the Covid-19 crisis broke in 2019, the WHO had quickly set up response systems, information exchange networks and had a good working relation with NGOs. The rapid response was largely made possible due to the experiences with earlier pandemics. But this time the WHO was much less successful in its role as international coordinator. There are many explanations for this, but prominent among them was the position taken by most Western countries. They felt confident they had the best health care systems in the world and therefore were disinclined to pass that part of their sovereignty on to the WHO. They preferred to close the borders and retreat in isolationism. While this may be considered the natural reaction of communities in times of crisis, the result was a break with international solidarity which had been the main driver of international politics for so long. It is yet another example of multilateralism being replaced by unilateralism, based on the assumption that national action serves the national interests better than international cooperation. Covid-19 did not cause this way of thinking but merely enforced it: countries with these unilateral political views already had policies in place to keep out international influences as much as possible, whether it was foreign culture, immigrants or the authority of international organizations.

Still, the issue at hand here is public health. National health care systems provide services to individuals and their individual needs. The unique feature of epidemics is that it affects everyone in the same measure. The prevention of such outbreaks requires nation-wide programs of vaccination or, if the outbreak has occurred, nation-wide measures. A similar situation is playing out on a world scale. When a pandemic hits the world, it doesn't matter that one country has its health care system in order and the other doesn't, because both countries will be equally affected by the disease. Of course, every state has a national responsibility of health care towards its population. But this will not suffice during a pandemic, and some type of international health care will then also be needed. This requires a vision that is multi-dimensional, covering the local, national and global at the same time. It remains to be seen, therefore, if the unilateralist tendencies of the Covid-19 pandemic will persist, or whether the pandemic will prompt states to embrace multilateralism in preparing for the next pandemic.

Further reading

Mika Aaltola, *Understanding the Politics of Pandemic Emergencies in the time of COVID-19. An Introduction to Global Politosomatics*, Routledge 2022

David P. Fidler, 'COVID-19 Pandemic, Geopolitics, and International Law, *Journal of International Humanitarian Legal Studies*, December 2020

Jin Un Kim, Obinna Oleribe, Ramou Njie & Simon D Taylor-Robinson, 'A time for new north–south relationships in global health, *International Journal of General Medicine*, 2017, pp.401-408

Kelley Lee, *The World Health Organization (WHO)*, Routledge, 2008

Richard Parker and Dulce Ferraz, 'Politics and pandemics', *Global Public Health*, 16 (2021), 1131-1140

Adam Roberts, *Pandemics and Politics*, Routledge, 2021

CHAPTER 7

Postcolonialism and decolonization

The term postcolonialism has acquired several meanings. In this textbook, two are considered of importance. The first meaning refers to the period and experiences of a former colonized country after colonialism. In African and Asian countries, for instance, postcolonialism represented the process of acquiring self-rule and an identity after the end of colonial rule. The processes of postcolonialism across the world took different forms because the colonial situations differed between countries and even continents: the practices and impacts of colonialism in Africa were different from those in Asia, and yet more different from those in South America (where indigenous populations were eradicated as a result of colonialism and, while Spanish rule may have ended, the Spanish settlers and former rulers never left) and North America (where the impact of settlers on the native population was combined with a massive import of enslaved people from Africa). But postcolonialism also has another meaning, namely, the impact that colonial structures and ways of thinking still have on today's world.

To address these challenges, it is said that 'decolonization' needs to take place, in other words: to undo the lingering effects of colonization, whether in a country that has been colonized, or in the world of today. Decolonization can be considered a global challenge, because it cannot be solved by only the communities who are affected by it, nor only by the communities that had caused it. For this, concerted efforts are needed that address the two (interconnected) types of postcolonialism, namely, the impact of colonialism on nation-building by former colonies and on their participation in the international domain, on the one hand, and, on the other, the impact on (academic) ways of understanding the world and one's position in that world. Decolonization therefore has a socio-political and an epistemological dimension. Both will be discussed below.

Two meanings of postcolonialism
Postcolonialism can mean 1) the period and experiences of a former colonized country after colonialism, and 2) the impact that colonial structures and ways of thinking still have on today's world.

Global challenge (1): socio-political 'decolonization'

Decolonization originally meant that the former colonized country was to reshape itself into a self-governing entity whereby its political, economic, educational, and other state systems were now under its own direction. In doing so, most former colonized countries have retained aspects of their former colonizer that usually consist of the legal or political system, state institutions, the language, or various cultural influences. Later – the 1990s are usually considered the starting point – the term 'decolonization' was also used to indicate the need of a former colonized society to forswear any political, social, cultural, linguistic, or intellectual legacy of its colonial past. In its extreme form, decolonization was a call to remove these remnants of the colonial past in their entirety and replace them with an indigenous legacy. Critics of this type of decolonization, themselves from former colonial countries, have pointed out that foreign influences can very well have become an integral part of the identity of the former colony and its people and should be accepted as such.

> ### Noble prize for Nigerian author Wole Soyinka
> The Nigerian author Wole Soyinka writes in the language of the colonizer (English) about (former colonized) Yoruba folklore in Nigerian everyday life of today. In 1986 he accepted the prestigious Nobel prize for literature from a Western country (Sweden) while wearing his national costume. At the ceremony in Stockholm, he had requested music to be played by a Nigerian composer (Fela Sowande) who writes music with the syntax of the colonizer (European classical music) for songs from Yoruba culture.

In either of these interpretations of 'decolonization', there remains a challenge to see what exactly is to be understood by decolonization, if it is warranted, and how it can be achieved. In doing so, many perceive this to be a global challenge, that is, a process that needs all (historical) parties involved to work together. If, on the other hand, this effort to decolonize is directed towards unilateral action by societies and countries to decolonize themselves, then it becomes justified to speak of a national, and perhaps regional, rather than a global challenge.

Multipolarization and the global South
The effects of a colonial past are not only felt by individual countries and their societies, they are also a legacy that these countries share. This is one of the reasons these countries are collectively referred to as the 'global South'. For most of these countries, however, colonialism is not a thing of the past: its structures are perceived as still present in the world today. Some see this in the advanced

economic position of Western countries compared to the global South, and they therefore advocate equity rather than equality. Others see the preservation of the colonial past in certain global structures that are remnants of colonial times, when the West had the power to design and impose these structures. One example is the UN Security Council, where the five permanent seats are held by the United States, the United Kingdom, France, Russia, and China (and each retains veto power). In 2017, 120 (of the 193) countries expressed their commitment to the reforms proposed by the UN Secretary-General in the UN General Assembly, but it remains to be seen if and how these reforms will be implemented.

> The lack of permanent seats for Latin America and Africa on the UN Security Council is "an unacceptable echo of domination from the colonial past"
> *(President Lula (Brazil), speech before UN General Assembly, September 2024)*

Since the 1990s, the antagonism between the global North and the global South has been increasingly expressed by the countries of the global South in policies that seek to move them away from political or economic dependence on Western countries. At the same time, fractures are emerging within the global North, with the United States pursuing an increasingly isolationist course. As a result, the structure of hegemonic 'blocs' (United States - Soviet Union during the Cold War period, America - Russia - China since the 2000s, but also global North - global South) is fragmenting into states opting for ad hoc relationships rather than subscribing to a single power 'bloc'. This development is called **multipolarization**, which is a combination of two interacting developments: on the one hand, the power of multiple actors (states, but also powerful individuals and corporations) to influence global events, and on the other hand, the growing antagonism among these actors. For some observers, this is the result of the end of the Cold War, when the bi-polar hegemony represented by the United States and the Soviet Union collapsed. Other observers see multipolarization as a result of the post-colonial antagonism between the global North and South, pitting the former colonized against the former colonizers.

An example of this multipolarization is how Russia and China are positioning themselves as competitors to the West - not only economically and technologically, but also in terms of values. A similar development is the formation of the BRICS in 2009: Brazil, Russia, India, China and South Africa created an alternative to the (Western) G7. All of these member states see multipolarization as a positive situation, albeit for different reasons: Brazil has stated that multipolarity is not anti-Western, but critical of Western domination; India claims the freedom to keep all options open and not to belong to any political camp; China sees BRICS as a counterweight to the G7; and Russia advocates a multipolar order in which not states but 'civilizational states' are entitled to sovereignty. Clearly, pragmatism, opportunism and sentiment all play a role in the multipolarization trend.

> **Multipolarization**
>
> "It has become a truism of foreign policy debates that the world is becoming ever more 'multipolar'. While the extent to which today's world is already multipolar is debatable, the world's 'multipolarization' is a fact: On the one hand power is shifting towards a larger number of actors who have the ability to influence key global issues. On the other hand, the world is experiencing increasing polarization both between and within many states, which is hampering joint approaches to global crises and threats."
>
> *(Multipolarization, Munich Security Report 2025)*

Multipolarization appears to be a new global trend, but is it also a global challenge? For those who have traditionally held most of the power, it certainly is. For example, the United States has reasserted itself against emerging political and economic powers like Russia and China. Since 2025, this policy has been dramatically intensified and accelerated under the Trump presidency. Multipolarization is also seen as a global challenge by those who believe in multilateralism and the rule-based global environment created by the many international agreements. Both the international cooperation and its legal infrastructure are undermined by the second dimension of multipolarization, that is: antagonism among actors, which creates a global environment in which national interests are pursued unilaterally, often in defiance of international rules. Finally, there are those who see the global trend toward multipolarization not as a challenge but as an opportunity because it allows smaller states to create their own network of alliances and cooperation without having to side with a single powerful entity.

Global challenge (2): epistemological 'decolonization'

Postcolonialism in academic thought seeks to answer the questions of 'How do formerly colonized peoples write their own histories and construct their own identities'. The reason for asking these questions is the realization that the way in which peoples from former colonized countries think about themselves, and structure their thought processes, is often defined by the epistemologies of Western thought. It is argued that the Western knowledge production and frames of thought continue to be perpetuated at the national and international levels across the globe: in politics, law, historical perceptions, and the structuring of states and educational institutions. As a result, the ways in which certain global structures have been shaped in the twentieth century are being called into question, like the economy (why only capitalism, when Islamic or Chinese concepts of economy might pose interesting alternatives?) or the organization of states (why do only five states have permanent seats with veto power in the United Nations?) or human rights (why only address the rights of the individual and not that of communities?). In addressing these questions, some call for the undoing of the domination of Western epistemologies, while others argue for a diversity of epistemologies whereby the Western epistemologies are not removed but included.

'Decoloniality'

Coloniality is a term that addresses the nexus of power and knowledge, arguing that most knowledge production is done in the global North and that this knowledge has global impact. Decoloniality stands for opening this knowledge monopoly up for other types of thinking, believing and living.

'Great African History'

In the 1960s, several leaders of newly independent African countries decided that, after the decolonization of their countries, they also wanted to decolonize their histories by rewriting it. UNESCO was put in charge of this historiographical project called 'Great African History'. Over 350 – mostly African scholars – were assembled to work on the numerous volumes that are still being published.

'De-colonizing' universities

Western-style universities and educational systems are dominant in most non-Western parts of the world: either as a residual legacy of Western education in colonized lands, or because former colonial states have reproduced these educational systems when establishing their own universities. Critics argue that such a university system still preserves knowledge and structures of thought that are inherently Western – and, according to some, colonial – in nature. Decolonizing universities can therefore mean two things: some argue that the Western-based epistemologies and curriculums need to be entirely replaced by indigenous ones, others call for widening them by including other epistemologies and curriculums.

> **Two views on 'decolonizing' universities**
>
> "A decolonized university in Africa should put African languages at the center of its teaching and learning project. The African university of tomorrow will be multilingual. It will teach (in) Swahili, Zulu, Xhosa, Shona, Yoruba, Hausa, Lingala, Gikuyu and it will teach all those other African languages that French, Portuguese or Arabic have become, while making a space for Chinese, Hindi etc. Decolonizing an African university requires a geographical imagination that extends well beyond the confines of the nation-state."
> *(Achille Joseph Mbembe, 'Decolonizing the university: New directions,' 2016)*
>
> Don't create another genre, but expand the existing epistemology, make it better. Just like feminism has not 'de-masculated' universities, but 'feminized' them.
> *(Olúfémi Táíwò, Against Decolonisation, 2022)*

Calls for decolonization can also be heard in Western universities. Some critics are concerned that the perpetuation of an academic tradition in which Western worldviews, knowledge, and theories dominate, is a continuation of colonial thinking. Others are concerned that such a tradition leaves little or no room for other perspectives or approaches. This is considered problematic because it may prevent the Western-trained viewer from seeing other viewpoints, structures, or epistemologies. For example, academic perspectives or theories that are perfectly valid in a Western context may make little sense when applied to non-Western contexts, thereby leaving the researcher with a flawed understanding of the topic at hand (see chapter 'Diversity').

Colonial and Postcolonial Studies
Colonial Studies study the histories and practices of colonialism. Postcolonial Studies take a critical view of Western academic approaches towards non-Western cultures and societies and tries to come up with alternative academic approaches.

These criticisms have proven to be valid, and many Western universities are attempting to come to a broader academic perspective on the methods and theories of academic study. These efforts have generated two discussions within the – mostly Western – university communities. One discussion is between those who advocate a broadening of worldviews, on the one hand, and those who argue that universities in Western countries should continue to teach the great books and thinkers of Western civilization, on the other. The second discussion is between those who want to expand existing Western knowledge production and theories with those from other cultures (thereby expanding the academic epistemology), and those who think that Western knowledge production and theories are essentially false and should be the source of criticism. These discussions are ongoing in the universities. Students of International Studies, by the very nature of their studies, will encounter them constantly. While the discussions may become polarizing, the important rule of thumb for any student should be: 'How can I get the broadest and best view of the topic that I am studying?'

'Universities are the enemy'

The perceived threat of universities as holders and producers of knowledge is not an exclusive post-colonial concern, but also of those who oppose the ideas of post-colonialism:

"Universities control the knowledge in our societies and what we call truth and falsity. They provide research that gives credibility to some of the most ridiculous ideas in our country. (...) If we want to do any of the things we want to do for our country and for the people who live in it, we have to honestly and aggressively attack the universities in this country."

J.D. Vance keynote address at the second National Conservatism Conference, 11 February 2021

(Vance is a Yale-graduate and vice-president under Donald Trump's 2025 presidency).

Communities and peoples

Among some minority communities, like the Muslims in Europe and indigenous peoples in North America and Australia, movements are emerging that claim their own epistemological way of thinking about themselves. This is a response to the majority view of societies in which they live, which has been imposed on these communities. One of the first steps in these processes is the use of one's own name and one's own language: not 'Indians' but Cheyenne or Iroquois, not 'Berber' but Amazigh, not 'Eskimo' but Innuit. Another step is that these peoples acknowledge their own history, especially in light of the historical narrative of the society and country that has subjugated, marginalized and sometimes even erased these peoples.

While this is one way to correct historical wrongs, another way for some peoples and communities is to look forward, reclaiming their own authentic ways of thinking about humanity and the world. For example, some First Nation people in America hold an integrated view of humanity and their environment. Similarly, some Muslim movements advocate a cosmic worldview of global human wellbeing based on Islamic principles. In some communities this type of thinking has taken the form of "Futurism", in which people break away from existing frameworks for thinking and develop their own, based on their own narratives, traditions and epistemologies. The aim of such thinking is, in the words of one of these thinkers: "to create a distinct future where we are not dependent on the gatekeepers to open the gate, and where we are not required, even to storm those gates, or to go around them."* As we have seen before, imagination is an important element of this type of future thinking.

Implications of 'decolonization' for land rights and self-government

In 1879, the Murray Islands of the coast of Australia were annexed by the British with the legal justification that these lands were 'no-man's land' (*terra nullius*). In the 1992 ruling Mabo v. State of Queensland, a majority of the court abandoned the doctrine of terra nullius. One reason was that this doctrine was considered legally contradicting, because it made the Aboriginal people of those islands 'intruders in their own homes'. Another reason was that this doctrine was considered unjust. As a result, the British common law of land rights was declared non-applicable the inhabitants of these islands were restored to their own inherent rights to land. The ongoing discussion among lawyers is now if this reasoning would also apply to inherent rights to self-government.

Further reading

Arjun Appadurai, 'Beyond Domination. The future and past of decolonization', *The Nation*, Vol.29 (22 March), 2021

Andrew Hurrell and Sandeep Sengupta, 'Emerging powers, North–South relations and global climate politics', *International Affairs*, Vol.88, No.3, 2012

L. Krüger, 'North-North, North-South and South-South Relations', in: *Encyclopedia of Life Support Systems, Vol.1: Global Transformations and World Futures*, 2009

Walter D. Mignolo, 'Delinking. The rhetoric of modernity, the logic of coloniality and the grammar of de-coloniality', *Cultural Studies*, 21 (2007), p.449-514

Sheila Nair, *Introducing Postcolonialism in International Relations Theory*, E-IR Foundation, 2017

David Slater, *Geopolitics and the Post-Colonial: Rethinking North-South Relations*, John Wiley & Sons, 2008

Olúfémi Táíwò, *Against Decolonisation. Taking African agency seriously*, Hurst Publishers, 2022

---

* Jason Edward Lewis, "The future imaginary", in *The Routledge Handbook of CoFuturisms*, Taryne Jade Taylor, Isiah Lavender III, Grace L. Dillon, and Bodhisattva Chattopadhyay (eds.) (London: Routledge, 2024), pp. 11-22.

Illustration Credits

PART I

3. Third perspective: the contemporary

I.3.1 World population growth
Retrieved from https://ourworldindata.org/population-growth-over-time
Made by Max Roser and Hannah Ritchie, reprinted under creative commons license CC-BY

I.3.2 Literacy rate
Retrieved from https://ourworldindata.org/grapher/cross-country-literacy-rates
Data source: World Bank (2024); Various sources (2018), reprinted under creative commons license
   CC-BY

5. Fifth perspective: diversity

I.5.1 World map
Retrieved from https://openclipart.org/detail/265865/world-map-in-oblique-cylindrical-equal-area
   -projection-with-graticule#google_vignette
Made by Ramiro Gómez (@gmz), Open Clip Art, public domain

PART II

1. Beliefs and belief systems

II.1.1 Separating religion and society
Design and copyright Maurits Berger

II.1.2 President Trump and religious community leaders
Retrieved from https://www.gettyimages.nl/detail/nieuwsfoto%27s/president-donald-trump-vice
   -president-mike-pence-and-nieuwsfotos/841608592
Made by Alex Wong / Staf, Getty Images North America.

2. Economics

II.2.1 China Belt and Road Initiative
Retrieved from https://merics.org/en/tracker/mapping-belt-and-road-initiative-where-we-stand
Made by MERICS (Mercator Institute for China Studies).

3. Nation and state

II.3.1 The increase in number of states in the world
Design and copyright Maurits Berger. Source: IOM, *World Migration Report*, 2024

II.3.2 Aboriginal plants flag in England
Retrieved from https://www.alamy.com/stock-photo-aboriginie-burnum-burnum-stakes-his-claim-on
-england-by-planting-his-106533660.html?imageid=1235AC90-9E3C-485A-A8D0-26656A72689F&p
=308342&pn=1&searchId=77daa07d44e7d94243c23eb9cb8c21a0&searchtype=0)
Made by PA Images, rights purchased from Alamy Stock photo

4. Non-state actors

II.4.1 Transnational organized crime
Retrieved from https://sherloc.unodc.org/cld/en/education/tertiary/organized-crime/module-5/
key-issues/measuring-product-markets.html
Source: *The Globalization of Crime: A Transnational Organized Crime Threat Assessment*, UNODC, 2010,
p.2.

7. Migration

II.7.1 Migration in the world
Design and copyright Maurits Berger. Source: IOM, *World Migration Report*, 2024

PART III
1. Power changes

III.1 Warrior king
Retrieved from https://www.flickr.com/photos/rietje/6396728661/
Made by Rita Willaert, reprinted under creative commons license CC BY-NC-SA 2.0

III.1 Kim Jong-un (North Korea)
Retrieved from https://www.afpforum.com/AFPForum/Search/Results.aspx?pn=1&smd=8&mui=3&q=
5548692027896193487_0&fst=kim+jong-un+horse&ft0=3&t=2&cck=a1aff2#
Photo released from the Korean Central News Agency

III.1 Vladimir Putin (Russia)
Retrieved from https://www.gettyimages.be/detail/nieuwsfoto%27s/russian-prime-minister-vladimir
-putin-rides-a-horse-nieuwsfotos/136334127?adppopup=true
Made by Alexsey Druginyn/AFP, rights purchased via Getty Images

III.1 Margaret Thatcher (United Kingdom)
Retrieved from https://www.gettyimages.nl/detail/nieuwsfoto%27s/conservative-party-
politician-and-prime-minister-of-the-nieuwsfotos/1466759752?adppopup=true Made by Peter
Jordan/Popperfoto / Contributor, rights purchased via Getty Images

III.1 George W. Bush (United States)
Retrieved from https://georgewbush-whitehouse.archives.gov/news/releases/2003/05/images/200305
   01-15_d050103-2-664v.html
Made by Susan Sterner, White House photo, public domain

2. Identity

III.2.1 Huntingtons' classification of 'civilizations'
Retrieved from https://commons.wikimedia.org/wiki/File:Clash_of_Civilizations_world_map.png
Made by Vardion and adapted by E Pluribus Anthony and unknown author, reprinted under creative
   commons license CC-BY-SA-3.0

3. Secularization and religionization

III.3.1 Equality and equity
Retrieved from https://commons.wikimedia.org/wiki/File:Equality_vs_Equity.png
Made by Ciell, reprinted under creative commons license CC BY-SA 4.0

4. Equality and self-determination

III.4.1 Students in Kabul, Afghanistan, 1972
Retrieved from https://www.gettyimages.be/detail/nieuwsfoto%27s/women-in-afghanistan-1972
   -young-students-wearing-mini-nieuwsfotos/1290037170?adppopup=true
Made by Laurence Brun, Gamma Rapho, rights purchased via Getty Images

III.4.2 Global growth of religion
Retrieved from https://www.pewresearch.org/religion/wp-content/uploads/sites/7/2022/12/3.png
Made by Pew Research Center, public domain

III.4.3 Global experience of religiosity
https://preview.redd.it/why-is-religion-still-so-important-in-our-country-vo-fkusmz35radd1.
   jpeg?width=559&format=pjpg&auto=webp&s=242458bd7537f52ea45b6502094d4414cbe14d22
Made by OpenStreetMap, public domain

5. Transnationalism

III.5.1 Transnationalism
Design and copyright Maurits Berger

PART IV

1. Information and communication

IV.0.1 Nexus 'migration'
Design and copyright Maurits Berger

IV.1.1 Public diplomacy
Design and copyright Maurits Berger

3. Resources and climate

IV.3.1 Nexuses 'climate change'
Design and copyright Maurits Berger

5. Unwanted migration

IV.5.1 Nexus migration - economy
Design and copyright Maurits Berger

IV.5.2 Nexus migration - security
Design and copyright Maurits Berger

Index

Printed in the United States
by Baker & Taylor Publisher Services